2 CORINTHIANS:
DISPENSATIONALLY CONSIDERED

A GRACE EXPOSITIONAL COMMENTARY

SECOND EDITION

DR. DAVID ALAN GREENE

GraceWord Publishing, LLC
www.gracewordpublishing.com
U.S.A.

GRACEWORD PUBLISHING

Contents

To My Dad Harold Alan Greene

Therefore
if any man be in Christ,
he is a new creature:
old things are passed away;
behold, all things are become new.

- Apostle Paul

Acknowledgements

I would like to express my appreciation to Jon and Susan McMahon who continually encourage me in my writing. My gratitude is due to Rev. Steven Tackett who is always willing to discuss the biblical text. Finally, a special thanks to Barbara Pennington, Frances Greene, and Janice Jewell who assisted me in the editing process.

Introduction

There is an approach to understanding Scripture that puts the entire Bible into a simple system of interpretation. The argument is that to understand God's Word we must reason from the general to the specific and not from the specific to the general. To choose only parts of Paul's epistles, here and there, and read them apart from their biblical context gets people into trouble with their interpretation. Looking at specific verses, detached from the general structure or framework of Scripture, is bad.

God created a timeline or eternal plan for the restoration of His Creation. This plan is first mentioned in Genesis. It is the *protoevangelium* or the first announcement of good news. God speaks to the Serpent or Satan in verse 3:15:

> 15 **And I will put enmity between thee [the Serpent] and the woman, and between thy seed and <u>her seed</u>; it [her seed] shall bruise thy head, and thou**

shalt bruise his heel.

Think about this. The word *seed* can be either singular or plural. The children of Abraham believe they are the *seed* of Abraham. That is quite true. However, in these verses, its use is singular and refers specifically to *the Seed,* Who is Christ. Also, notice that it is the woman's seed because it was given to her by God directly. This is often called the *immaculate conception* or the divine impregnation of the virgin Mary by the Holy Spirit. This is the holy *Seed.* The above verse is the very first promise of good news and it remains the central theme throughout the entire Bible! This theme is said to be like a scarlet thread woven throughout Scripture. Christ is this *Seed.* It is He Who will ultimately redeem Creation!

God does things methodically. He patiently works His plan of restoration and makes Himself known to man through a series of progressive revelations. Timothy was a student preacher trained by Paul. His letters to both Timothy and Titus are referred to as the *pastoral epistles* because they instruct these young pastors. Paul wants Timothy to understand Scripture and teach it correctly. Following Paul's instructions, he will be neither ashamed nor embarrassed. 2 Timothy 2:15:

15 **Study to shew thyself approved unto**

God, a workman that needeth not to be ashamed, <u>rightly dividing the word of truth</u>.

The Greek word translated as *rightly dividing* is *orthotomeo*. It is a compound word comprised of *ortho* which mean *correct* or *with great precision* and the word *tomeo* which is the verb *to cut*. A similar example would be *orthodox*. Again, *ortho* means *correct* or *with great precision* and *dox* means *doctrine* or *teaching*. When combined *orthodox* means *correct doctrine*. The last example is a medical procedure which includes the cutting out or removal of something. In its medical name, the suffix *-ectomy* is added. The Greek *ek* which means *out* is attached to the verb *tomeo* means *to cut out*. This is a lot of detail to make an important point. Paul is instructing Timothy to carefully and correctly *cut* or *divide* the *Word of Truth.* By doing so, he will not be ashamed before man or before God.

Therefore, this concept of *carefully dividing Scripture*, when applied correctly, makes a huge difference on its interpretation! As with most things, the Bible is the sum of its *parts*. These *parts* or *divisions* of the Bible are called *dispensations*. In Greek, the word for *dispensation* is *oikonomia*. This is also a compound word. It is comprised of *oikos* meaning *household* and *nomos* meaning *law or rule*. *Oikonomia* is the origin of our word *economy*. A president rules or administers his country and its economy by certain laws. Therefore, a *dispensation* is a period of time, or an age, in which God *dispenses* or administrates His household.

This brief summary of *dispensation* does not do it justice. For a deeper explanation, I would recommend you read *Letters To Theophilus* which handles the subject in greater detail. It explains all seven dispensations in God's plan for restoration. There are two dispensations which are critical to our understanding of Corinthians. Presently, we are in what many call the *Church Age*. I do not like this name because the word *church* has too many uses. I prefer the name *Age of Grace*. This better reflects the means by which God currently administers His creation. Friend, salvation by *grace* without works is the very foundation of Paul's messages.

Paul is the only one who uses the word *dispensation* in the Bible. Here are the four verses:

1 Corinthians 9:17:

> 17 **For if I do this thing willingly, I have a reward: but if against my will, <u>a dispensation of the gospel is committed unto me.</u>**

Ephesians 1:10:

10 That in <u>the dispensation of the ful-ness of times</u> he might gather together in one all things in Christ, both which are in heaven, and which are on earth; even [that is to say] in him:

Ephesians 3:2:

2 If ye have heard of <u>the dispensation of the grace of God</u> which is given me to you-ward [for you]:

Colossians 1:25:

25 Whereof I am made a minister, ac-cording to <u>the dispensation of God</u> which is given to me for you, to fulfil the word of God;

These verses should not be interpreted out of context. They are solely presented here as evidence of Paul's use of the word *dispensation* in his epistles.

Many dispensational theologians have *divided* the Bible into seven divisions. Is it not interesting that this is the same number of days in Creation? For the purpose of our study, we will concentrate on only two dispensations. They are the *Age of Law* and the *Age of Grace*. Under the Mosaic Covenant, Israel obligated itself to the keeping of the Law. The weight of the Law proved to be too much for them. The Gentiles, or non-Jews, who were outside of the commonwealth of Israel were not part of this covenantal agreement. They were strangers from God and followed after false gods.

In Acts 2, Peter makes an impassioned speech on Pentecost to the Jews celebrating their holiday in Jerusalem. The Jews had rejected and crucified their Messiah. At the end of the book of Acts, Paul makes a proclamation. Acts 28:28-29:

> 28 **Be it known therefore unto you, that the salvation of God is sent unto the Gentiles, and that they will hear it.**
>
> 29 **And when he had said these words, the Jews departed, and had great reasoning among themselves.**

The thirteen epistles or letters which immediately follow Acts were written by the Apostle Paul. Each letter is written to a group of believers or specific individuals such as Philemon, Titus, and Timothy. All of his letters, with the exception of Romans, were written to people Paul had met personally. Many of whom he lived with while teaching them face to face. Therefore, most recipients of these letters had a general understanding of his doctrine before receiving his letter.

The letter to the Romans is different. Some had heard Paul and believed. Then, they relocated to the capitol city of Rome. Many who had not met or heard Paul teach had become believers solely by the testimony of others. Romans was written to provide the foundational basis of Paul's doctrine. Upon this, all his other letters are written. It was for this reason that it is placed first in the series of his epistles.

I like to use this as an example. Take a moment and think about a multi-part series of an epic story. How difficult it is to understand the full depth of the story by starting in the middle? It would be difficult to understand it. For this same reason, we must consider the unique gospel message preached by Paul as a whole. We must not confuse or combine his distinct message with the message preached by the Twelve!

The Apostle Paul preached a different gospel message than the Twelve. Scripture confirms that he personally received this from the Risen Savior. The information he received was a mystery and, therefore, had never been disclosed to anyone until it was disclosed to him. Furthermore, this gospel message which Paul received was specifically directed to the

Gentiles. Let us consider the evidence.

Scripture records his confrontation with the Risen Savior on the Road to Damascus in Acts 9:3-9:

> 3 And as he journeyed, he came near Damascus: and suddenly there shined round about him a light from heaven:
> 4 And he fell to the earth, and heard a voice saying unto him, Saul, Saul, why persecutest thou me? 5 And he said, <u>Who art thou, Lord?</u> And the Lord said, <u>I am Jesus whom thou persecutest</u>: it is hard for thee to kick against the pricks.
>
> 6 And he trembling and astonished said, Lord, what wilt thou have me to do? And the Lord said unto him, Arise, and go into the city, and it shall be told thee what thou must do.
>
> 7 And the men which journeyed with him stood speechless, hearing a voice, but seeing no man. 8 And Saul arose from the earth; and when his eyes were opened, he saw no man: but they led him by the hand, and brought him into Damascus. 9 And he was three days without sight, and neither did eat nor

drink.

The Apostle Paul had never met Jesus in person during His earthly ministry. Therefore, he could not fulfill the requirements for the replacement of Judas as the twelfth apostle. (*cf.* Acts 1:21-26.)

In Damascus, God directs a faithful disciple named Ananias to heal Paul's blindness. Pay close attention to the evidence presented in this dialogue between God and Ananias. Acts 9:10-16

> 10 **And there was a certain disciple at Damascus, named Ananias; and to him said the Lord in a vision, Ananias. And he said, Behold, I am here, Lord.** 11 **And the Lord said unto him, Arise, and go into the street which is called Straight, and enquire in the house of Judas for one called Saul, of Tarsus: for, behold, he prayeth,** 12 **And hath seen in a vision a man named Ananias coming in, and putting his hand on him, that he might receive his sight.**
>
> 13 **Then Ananias answered, Lord, I have heard by many of this man, <u>how much evil he hath done to thy saints at Jerusalem</u>:**

14 And here he hath authority from the chief priests to bind all that call on thy name.

15 But the Lord said unto him, <u>Go thy way: for he is a chosen vessel unto me, to bear my name before the Gentiles, and kings, and the children of Israel:</u> 16 <u>For I will shew him how great things he must suffer for my name's sake.</u>

Later, in his letter to the Galatians, Paul wrote something he most likely shared with others in person. The following verses recount his second meeting with the other apostles in Jerusalem. Paul met only Peter and James on his first trip to Jerusalem fourteen years prior. Galatians 2:1-9:

1 Then fourteen years after I went up again to Jerusalem with Barnabas, and took Titus with me also. 2 And I went up by revelation, and communicated unto them that gospel which I preach among the Gentiles, but privately to them which were of reputation, lest [for fear that] by any means I should run, or had run, in vain.

3 But neither Titus, who was with me,

being a Greek, was compelled to be circumcised: 4 And that because of false brethren unawares brought in, who came in privily to spy out our liberty which we have in Christ Jesus, that they might bring us into bondage: 5 To whom we gave place by subjection, no, not for an hour; that the truth of the gospel might continue with you.

6 But of these who seemed to be somewhat [of importance], (whatsoever they were, it maketh no matter to me: God accepteth no man's person:) for they who seemed to be somewhat in conference added nothing to me:

7 But contrariwise, when they saw that the gospel of the uncircumcision was committed unto me, as the gospel of the circumcision was unto Peter; 8 (For he that wrought effectually in Peter to the apostleship of the circumcision, the same was mighty in me toward the Gentiles:) 9 And when James, Cephas, and John, who seemed to be pillars, perceived the grace that was given unto me, they gave to me and Barnabas the right hands of fellowship; that we should go

unto the heathen [Gentiles], and they unto the circumcision [Jews].

It is important for us to see the separation of their ministries here. The Twelve are taking their message to the Jews. Paul is taking his message to the Gentiles or non-Jews. This evidence is critical.

Paul provides a concise statement of his gospel here in 1 Corinthians. Notice, below, his use of the definite article *the* when referring to *the* gospel. Here, we find Paul's *Gospel of Grace* in its simplest form – the basis of his gospel message. 1 Corinthians 15:1-4:

1 **Moreover, brethren, I declare unto you the gospel which I preached unto you, which also ye have received, and wherein ye stand; 2 By which also ye are saved, if ye keep in memory what I preached unto you, unless ye have believed in vain.**

3 **For I delivered unto you first of all that which I also received, [1] how that Christ died for our sins according to the scriptures; 4 [2] And that he was buried, and [3] that he rose again the third day according to the scriptures:**

We must always remember the simplicity of the *Gospel of Grace*. It consists of Christ's death on the Cross, His burial, and His resurrection. It is *by faith* or *by believing these facts* that anyone can receive salvation! His death, burial, and resurrection allows God to *justify sinners!* Those who believe by faith are justified — are *proclaimed not guilty!* All this is possible because of what God accomplished through the completed work of His Son, Jesus Christ!

The sufficiency of Christ's completed work on the Cross is critical to the *Gospel of Grace*. This cannot be over emphasized. Nothing must be added. Nothing! There can be no additional requirements; no ordinances or laws. Paul makes this clear in all his letters. This is perhaps one of the most quoted verses from Paul's writings. Ephesians 2:8-9:

> 8 **For <u>by grace are ye saved</u> through faith; and that not of yourselves: <u>it is the gift of God</u>: 9 <u>Not of works</u>, lest [for fear that] any man should boast.**

In his letter to the Galatians, he chastised some of them because they had added works as a requirement for salvation. Today, many Christians still add the requirement of works to the simplicity of the gospel. Salvation is by grace, a gift, through faith which is believing! Paul gives this warning to the believers in Colossae. Colossians 2:8:

> **8 Beware lest any man spoil you through <u>philosophy</u> and <u>vain deceit</u>, after the <u>tradition of men</u>, after the <u>rudiments of the world</u>, and not after Christ.**

Paul's gospel message is separate and distinct from the Twelve. In Galatians. He confirms that he did not receive it from any of the other apostles or, for that matter, from any other man. He also confirms that he received it directly from the Risen Savior! Galatians 1:11-12:

> **11 But I certify you, brethren, that the gospel which was preached of [by] me is not after [from] man. 12 <u>For I neither received it of [from] man, neither was I taught it [by man], but by the revelation of [from] Jesus Christ.</u>**

When growing up I remember asking my Methodist pastor why he did not preach from Paul's letters. He told me that it was because Paul had persecuted the Church and, therefore, he was taught by his seminary to avoid him. Another pastor told me that Paul's writings were only his opinion and, therefore, not reliable. Friend, either Scripture is inspired, infallible, and complete or it is not. The Bible is our only source of truth. It is trustworthy. We have God's Word on it!

Paul was once an enemy of God. He admits this saying he persecuted the Kingdom Believers. Galatians 1:13-14:

> 13 **For ye have heard of my conversation [manner of living] <u>in time past in the Jews' religion, how that beyond measure I persecuted the church of God, and wasted it:</u>**
>
> 14 **And [I] profited in the Jews' religion above many my equals in mine own nation, being more exceedingly zealous of the traditions of my fathers.**

This is great news for people who, like me, are sinners. For if God can save Paul, then He can save me. He can save anyone who is willing to believe. Paul continues with verses 15-17:

> 15 **But <u>when it pleased God</u>, who separated me from my mother's womb, and called me by his grace,**
>
> 16 **<u>To reveal his Son in [to] me</u>, <u>that I might preach him among the heathen</u>**

[Gentiles]; immediately **I conferred not with flesh and blood** [any man]:

17 **Neither went I up to Jerusalem to them which were apostles before me;** but [instead] I went into Arabia, and [later] returned again unto Damascus.

God set Paul a part for a special ministry to the Gentiles. This did not mean that the offer of the *Gospel of Grace* was not also open to the Jews. It is available to everyone but it is only effective for those who believe. Throughout all his epistles, Paul teaches that *faith* or *believing God,* like Abraham, is the only basis for salvation. In Genesis, we are told that Abraham *believed* in the LORD and it was counted to him as *righteousness.* (*cf.* Gen. 15:6.)

Here is something that may help if you are new to this concept that Paul's gospel is different from the other Twelve. Find a large jumbo paper clip. Now, beginning with the last page of Acts and ending with the first page of Hebrews place the large paper clip over those pages in between. The pages contained within the paper clip should begin with Romans and end with Philemon. These are the thirteen epistles written by Paul. In a moment, you will see how this makes sense.

Now, take a look at the last chapter of Acts. These verses immediately precedes Paul's first book. When Paul is incarcerated in Rome, he calls the local Jewish leaders to meet with him. (*cf.* Acts 28:16-30.) After reasoning with them at great length, they leave undecided and are arguing amongst themselves. At this point, notice that Paul makes a declaration. This declaration was not only to these Jews. For the Gentiles, it is a very important flag signaling a dispensational change. Acts 28:28:

> 28 **Be it known therefore unto you, that <u>the salvation of God is sent unto the Gentiles</u>, and <u>that they will hear it</u>.**

Is it interesting that these are the words which end the portion of Scripture immediately preceding Paul's epistles? Now, let us go to the other side of the paperclip and look at the book which follows Paul's epistles. You should see the book of *Hebrews*. Are you seeing a pattern here yet? Hebrews is written to *believing Israel!* These are the Jewish believers who follow the teaching of the Twelve. They are following the *Gospel of the Kingdom* preached by Christ and the Twelve! Look at Peter's confession. Matthew 16:16:

> 16 **And Simon Peter answered and said, Thou art the Christ [Messiah], the Son of the living God.**

There is a huge error surrounding this conversation. I would like to pause for a moment and resolve it for you. Christ is God's Son Who will fulfill the promises made to the fathers: Abraham, Isaac, and Jabob. There is only one Christ. There is only one Crucifixion. However, it applies to the children of the promises one way and the Gentiles another. Here is Jesus' response to Peter's statement. Verses 17-18:

> 17 **And Jesus answered and said unto him, Blessed art thou, Simon Barjona: for flesh and blood hath not revealed it unto thee, but my Father which is in heaven.**

> 18 **And I say also unto thee, <u>That thou art Peter, and upon this rock I will build my church</u>; and the gates of hell shall not prevail against it.**

The Greek word used by Luke for *rock* is the feminine word (Gr: petra) and not the masculine word (Gr: petros). The church is not built on Peter, but upon the idea or concept stated by Peter in answer to Christ's question. I will finish with this. Christ's earthly ministry was to the lost sheep of the house of Israel only. (*cf.* Matt. 10:2-6, Rom. 15:8.)

The gospel which Paul received from the Lord

Jesus Christ is directed to the Gentiles! It is called *the Gospel of Grace* for a reason. *Grace* means *gift*. It is God's gift to anyone who, by *faith,* believes what God has already done for them. Because of His Son's death, burial, and resurrection, God is graciously offering salvation as a gift to anyone who believes. Why? It is because Christ paid the price in full!

Therefore, it is critical for us, as we seek to understand Paul's letters, that we understand the two dispensations involved. They are the *Age of Law* and the *Age of Grace*. Most pastors and teachers of the Bible believe that these two dispensations are sequential. In other words, they believe that one dispensation follows the other, but this is not true. The *Age of Law* began with Moses. Israel contractually accepted and, therefore, are bound by the Mosaic Covenant. This covenant was still in effect at the time of Jesus' ministry. Matthew 5:17

> 17 **Think not that I am come to destroy the law, or the prophets: <u>I am not come to destroy, but to fulfil [the Law].</u>**

However, Paul's message is different. It is about grace. Therefore, as grace believers, we must not mingle grace with the Law! He explains to the believers in Galatia why this is important. Galatians 2:21:

21 I do not frustrate the grace of God: for if righteousness come by the law, then Christ is dead in vain.

The *Age of Law* has been temporarily suspended. It will resume at the close of the *Age of Grace*. This is referred to as a *parenthetical interruption*. The prophetic program disclosed in Daniel 9 is currently held in abeyance until this present age, the *Age of Grace*, is completed. We are not introduced to Paul, named Saul, until the stoning of Stephen. Shortly after that, the *Age of Grace* began with the conversion of Paul. He was *the first to be saved by grace through faith*. The *Age of Grace* will end at *His Calling* of those saved by His grace through faith — the *Rapture*.

GraceWord Publishing has excellent books which explain *rightly dividing* in greater detail. As I mentioned before, the book entitled *Letters to Theophilus* is a summary of the entire Bible from Genesis to Revelation. On the other side of the coin, *The Glorious Destiny Of Israel* presents the promises and prophecies given exclusively to Israel.

With this introductory summary of the *Age of Grace* and Paul's unique gospel message, we are ready to begin our study of 2 Corinthians.

1

About Corinth

Let us start by finding Corinth on a map. By using the QR code provided below, you will see that it is located on an isthmus at the bottom of the Gulf of Corinth. It is due west of Athens by about 150 miles. You will also see Corinth's location relative to the cities of Ephesus and Thessaloniki. The first receiving one letter and the latter two letters from the Apostle Paul.

https://www.bibleodyssey.org/wp-content/uploads/2022/11/map-Corinth-spm-g-02.jpg

During the time of Paul, Corinth was one of the

larger and important cities in Greece. It had an estimated population, at that time, of 90,000. The city was destroyed by the Romans in 146 BC. Later, Julius Caesar would rebuild the city in 44 BC. Rome made Corinth the capital of this Grecian province.

Scholars place Paul's first visit to Corinth between 49 and 50 A.D. Prior to his visit, there had been trouble in Athens and he was sent away for his safety. Acts 18:1-5:

> 1 **After these things Paul departed from Athens, and came to Corinth; 2 And found a certain Jew named Aquila, born in Pontus, lately come from Italy, with his wife Priscilla; (because that Claudius had commanded all Jews to depart from Rome:) and came unto them.**
>
> 3 **And because he [Paul] was of the same craft, he abode with them, and wrought [worked]: for by their occupation they were tentmakers. 4 And he reasoned in the synagogue every sabbath, and persuaded the Jews and the Greeks. 5 And when Silas and Timotheus were [had] come from Macedonia, Paul was pressed in the spirit, and testified to the Jews that Jesus was Christ.**

Being moved by the Spirit to speak more boldly, the opposition increased. Yet, Paul continued to preach the Gospel of Grace unabated. Verses 6-8:

> 6 **And when they opposed themselves, and blasphemed, he shook his raiment, and said unto them, <u>Your blood be upon your own heads; I am clean: from henceforth I will go unto the Gentiles</u>.**
>
> 7 **And he departed thence, and entered into a certain man's house, named Justus, one that worshipped God, whose house joined hard to the synagogue.**
>
> 8 **And Crispus, the chief ruler of the synagogue, believed on the Lord with all his house; and many of the Corinthians hearing [also] believed, and were baptized.**

God assures Paul that no harm shall befall him. Verses 9-11:

> 9 **Then spake the Lord to Paul in the night by a vision, Be not afraid, but speak, and hold not thy peace: 10 For I am with thee, and no man shall set on**

thee to hurt thee: for I have much [many] people in this city.

11 And he [Paul] continued there a year and six months, teaching the word of God among them.

God called Paul to this apostleship. It is he who established the doctrinal foundation for grace believers. After their conversion, he maintains a relationship with them by writing letters to them. Seeing himself as the father of their faith, he continues to care for them as his children in the faith.

Most theologians date the first letter to the Corinthians as being written in 57 AD from Ephesus. Later, in 58 AD, he writes his second letter to them from Macedonia. Paul is making plans to visit Corinth again. He wants to see them face to face and enjoy their fellowship. He hopes he can spend the winter months with them strengthening them in the faith. Much of what is recorded in the Corinthian letters happens at the beginning of his missionary journeys. It is believed that during his winter sojourn there, he writes his letter to the believers in Rome.

Paul's letters to the Corinthians has both the sternness and the love of a father. There are major issues within the fellowship. He feels they must be

4

addressed before he comes in person. He mingles compassion with a warning. If they do not heed his advice, then, when he comes to them, he must do so with harshness and rebuke. Although some of them are as unrepentant children, Paul makes one thing crystal clear. God's love for them never changes! Their actions may have earthly consequences, but their eternal salvation, based upon genuine faith, remains secure *in Christ!*

2

2 Corinthians 1

Paul begins his letter with this salutation or greeting to the believers in Corinth. The letter was from the Apostle Paul. However, since Timothy is with him and known by the Corinthians, Paul includes him in his greeting. 2 Corinthians 1:1:

> 1 **Paul, an apostle of Jesus Christ by the will of God, and [along with] Timothy our brother, unto the church of God which is at Corinth, with all the saints which are in all Achaia:**

Paul was writing from Macedonia, the region north of Greece. His apostolic letters are valuable instruction from God and read aloud in the assemblies.

For some time, Paul knew there was trouble

within the Corinthian assembly from reports he received. Those that opposed faithful doctrine had entered the assemblies, risen to power, and were refuting both his teaching and authority as an apostle. Notice in his salutation he includes the phrase "Paul, an apostle of Jesus Christ by the will of God" (v. 1). He includes the following to remind them that they have received *grace* from God with His offer of amnesty. Through God's grace they can have *peace* with God through His Son Jesus Christ. Many will reject His gracious offer of peace. When the current Age of Grace ends, God will judge all who rejected His Son. Verse 2:

> 2 **Grace be to you and peace from God our Father, and from the Lord Jesus Christ.**

He reminds them that God the Father is the provider of comfort in trials and tribulations. It is with this same comfort we receive as believers that we are to comfort others with the hope we have in the gospel of our salvation. What hope? Spiritually, we are safe and secure in Christ. We are waiting for the promised redemption of our body. This is called the *Blessed Hope*. This is *His Calling* or the *Rapture*. Verses 3-4:

> 3 **Blessed be God, even [that is to say]**

the Father of our Lord Jesus Christ, the Father of mercies, and the God of all comfort;

4 Who comforteth us in all our tribulation, that we may be able to comfort them which are in any trouble, by the comfort wherewith we ourselves are comforted of God.

We suffer from these tribulations and troubles because we are believers and belong to God. Therefore, we are hated by *the world* which is governed by powers, principalities, and rulers of darkness. We know that darkness hates the light and, as the children of light, believers suffer on earth as did Christ. Verses 5-7:

5 For as the sufferings of Christ abound in us, so <u>our consolation also aboundeth by Christ</u>.

6 And whether we be afflicted, it is for your <u>consolation and salvation</u>, which is effectual in the enduring of the same sufferings which we also suffer: or whether we be comforted, it is for your <u>consolation and salvation</u>.

7 **And our hope of you is stedfast, know-ing, that as <u>ye are partakers of the suf-ferings, so shall ye be also of the conso-lation.</u>**

Paul explains to them the *consolation and salvation* which they have. The word *consolation* means *to comfort; alleviate from misery or distress of mind; to strengthen the mind or faith with hope, joy, and courage.*

In times of trouble, we all need comfort. However, since this is easily forgotten, Paul reminds them. Verses 8-9:

8 **For we would not, brethren, have you ignorant of our trouble which came to us in Asia, that we were pressed out of measure, above [beyond our] strength, insomuch that we despaired even of life:**

9 **But we had the sentence of death in ourselves, that we should not trust in ourselves, but in God which raiseth the dead:**

We must remember in Whom we have placed our trust. As we await our bodily redemption, our bodies, like all others, have been sentenced to death.

However, with the *blessed hope* of our bodily redemption, we know we will be delivered. Verses 10-11:

> 10 **[God] Who delivered us from so great a death, and doth deliver: in whom we trust that he will yet deliver us;**
>
> 11 **Ye also helping together by prayer for us, that for the gift bestowed upon us by the means of many persons thanks may be given by many on our behalf.**

Paul continues to suffer greatly throughout his ministry. Being human, he sometimes despairs to the point of wishing he was no longer alive but with Christ. Then, he remembers what he now tells us. We must not rely upon ourselves, but instead trust *in God Who raised Jesus from the dead*. When we do this, we can rejoice in our situation. Verse 12:

> 12 **For our rejoicing is this, the testimony of our conscience, that in simplicity and godly sincerity, not with fleshly wisdom, but by the grace of God, we have had our conversation [living] in the world, and more abundantly to youward.**

They are grace believers. Their consciences have

been taught the simplicity of God's salvation. They are not to rely on the knowledge of man, but instead upon their knowledge of God's grace! Paul uses the word *conversation* to mean their *manner of living* within this fallen world. Much of his life has been devoted to teaching and preaching for their benefit. However, like them, he also experiences the challenges of this world.

Paul seeks to make clear his doctrine whether in person or in his writings. He prays that they will hold onto what they have learned until the end. Paul writes these words to Timothy, his son in the faith. 2 Timothy 1:13-14:

> 13 **Hold fast the form of sound words, which thou hast heard of [from] me, in faith and love which is in Christ Jesus. 14 That good thing which was committed unto thee keep by the Holy Ghost which dwelleth in us.**

Paul rejoices in faithful believers who, like him, also rejoice unto the day of *His Calling*. Together, they share in the same rejoicing! Below, the *day of the Lord Jesus* is the *Calling of the Body of Christ unto Himself.* This is the Rapture! 2 Corinthians 1:13-14:

> 13 **For we write none other things [else]**

unto you, than what ye read or **acknowledge; and I trust ye shall acknowledge <u>even to [until] the end;</u>**

> **14 As also ye have acknowledged us in part, that we are your rejoicing, even [that is to say] as ye also are ours in <u>the day of the Lord Jesus.</u>**

Paul intends to come to them again so that he might encourage them and fill up their faith. He plans to visit them on his way from Macedonia to Jerusalem. He will bring offerings received amongst the grace assemblies for the Jews there. (*cf.* Gal. 2:10.) Verses 15-16:

> **15 And in this confidence I was minded to come unto you before, that ye might have a second benefit;**

> **16 And to pass by you into Macedonia, and to come again out of Macedonia unto you, and of [by] you to be brought on my way toward Judaea.**

The following verses require some explanation. It has to do with truth in brevity. In other words, he will be direct and not use many words. Jesus said, "But let your communication be, Yea, yea; Nay, nay:

for whatsoever is more than these cometh of evil" (Matt. 5:37). Paul is saying the same thing. When Paul set his mind to it, he wants to speak to them directly and not beat around the bush. Verse 17:

> 17 **When I therefore was thus minded, did I use lightness? or the things that I purpose, do I purpose according to the flesh, that with me there should be yea yea, and nay nay?**

This is also evident in 1 Corinthians. He did not use fleshly words to placate or appease them, but instead he came right to the point. He did not confuse them, but taught them the truth directly.

From him they had learned the unchanging promises of God *in Christ*. These promises were not yes or no. They were all *yea* or true! Verses 18-20:

> 18 **But as God is true, our word toward you was not yea and nay.**

> 19 **For the Son of God, Jesus Christ, who was preached among you by us, even by me and Silvanus and Timotheus, was not yea and nay, <u>but in him [Christ] was yea [true]</u>.**

20 For all the promises of God in him [Christ] are yea [true], and [are] in him [Christ] Amen, unto the glory of God by us.

Most Christians are familiar with the word *amen* which is used quite regularly in some congregations. By it, they are letting the speaker know they agree. Let us consider a deeper meaning. It means we confirm an established truth. It is something in which we can trust with complete confidence: *unto the glory of God by us.*

In the next verse, look at Who establishes us *in Christ!* It is God! Verse 21:

21 Now he which [Who] stablisheth us with you in Christ, and hath anointed us, is God;

I would like you to look at the verb tenses. One is the present tense, current, and the other is the past tense, completed. God is currently establishing us *in Christ.* Some people call that *sanctification* which is the process by which we are separated from the world. However, He has anointed us. That action is complete. It is a done deal. When we believed in His death, burial, and resurrection, we were redeemed. We were bought back from sin's condemnation. This transaction is a done deal!

Concerning this transaction, look at what Paul tells the grace believers. Ephesians 2:4-6:

> 4 **But God, who is rich in mercy, for <u>his great love wherewith he loved us</u>, 5 Even when we were dead in sins, <u>[God] hath [has] quickened us together with Christ</u>, (by grace ye are saved;)**
>
> 6 **And <u>hath raised us up together</u>, and <u>made us sit together in heavenly places in Christ Jesus</u>:**

All of the verbs in the above two verses are in the past tense. He saved us (past tense) while we were dead in our sins. He made us (past tense) alive with Christ. He has already accomplish everything necessary on our behalf. Spiritually, we remain seated in heaven *in Christ* awaiting our bodily redemption at *His Calling.* The completion of our redemption, our physical bodies, is guaranteed by the holy Spirit of Promise. (Read Ephesians 1:7-12.)

Friend, this is great news! The completion of our redemption is guaranteed. There are two words I want you to notice below: *sealed* and *earnest.* Then, I will explain them. 1 Corinthians 1:22:

22 Who <u>hath also sealed us</u>, and <u>given the earnest of the Spirit</u> in our hearts.

Let us compare this verse to Ephesians 1:13-14:

13 In whom ye also trusted, <u>after that ye heard the word of truth, the gospel of your salvation: in whom also after that ye believed, ye were sealed with that holy Spirit of promise,</u>

14 <u>Which is the earnest of our inheritance until the redemption of the purchased possession,</u> unto the praise of his glory.

I underlined almost the whole of these verses. It is so important that you understand this. When we hear and believe the gospel of our salvation, we are sealed. If you are saved by grace through faith, then you have been sealed. That is a done deal. We also received the holy Spirit of Promise Who resides in us. We were bought and paid for by His blood. When God looks at us, He sees the righteousness of Christ! Do not forget that.

The other important word is *earnest*. This is an old legal word still used in real estate transactions today. It is *the deposit which secures the completion of the promised transaction.* Paul tells us that grace believers are spiritual *in Christ* Who is seated in heaven beside the Father. However, physically, we remain here in our earthy body until the promised redemption. Our complete redemption, our inheritance, is guaranteed by the Holy Spirit. Here He is called the holy Spirit of Promise. He remains within us *until the redemption of the purchased possession.* Who is this purchased possession? We are! We were bought and paid for with the blood of Jesus Christ. We belong to God. The Holy Spirit guarantees the transaction will be completed. We have His Word on it!

Much of what is happening in the Corinthian assembly was not acceptable. Paul delayed his coming to them by choosing, instead, to first send them this letter. He is not looking to rule over them. Instead, he wants them to have joy! With all this incredible news, only their sin could prevent them from being filled with joy. Paul reminds them to hold firm to correct doctrine. Verses 23-24:

> 23 Moreover I call [on] God for a record upon my soul, that to spare you I came not as yet unto Corinth.

> 24 Not for that we have dominion over your faith, but [we] are <u>helpers of your joy: for by faith ye stand.</u>

3

2 Corinthians 2

We know the reason that Paul delayed his coming to Corinth. He was afraid it would distress both the believers and him. If he did come with rebuke, then from whom could they find encouragement and gladness? 2 Corinthians 1-2:

> 1 **But I determined this with myself, that I would not come again to you in heaviness. 2 For if I make you sorry, who is he then that maketh me glad, but the same which is made sorry by me?**

He is truly distressed over the news he is receiving about the state of their assembly. He writes to them so that they will correct the problem before he visits them in person. Verse 3:

3 And I wrote this same unto you, lest, when I came, I should have sorrow from them of whom I ought to rejoice; having confidence in you all, that my joy is the joy of you all.

The same believers who are to be a source of joy for him are causing him sorrow. However, he has confidence in them that they will change and his joy in them will return.

You can feel Paul's frustration and concern as a father for his children in the faith. In spite of their moral situation, he still loves them. Verse 4:

4 For out of much affliction and anguish of heart I wrote unto you with many tears; not that ye should be grieved, but that ye might know the love which I have more abundantly unto you.

He refers to the individual who sinned. He was only partially grieved. Paul knows the world and his expulsion from the assembly has remedied the situation. He does not want to disparage all of them simply because they are members of the same assembly. Verse 5:

5 But if any have caused grief, he hath

not grieved me, but in part: that I may not overcharge you all.

Once the unrepentant sinner was removed from the assembly, their health and safety were restored. However, it may surprise you to see how Paul shows concern for this individual sinner. As all sinners, he still should be forgiven and loved in hopes that he might be fully restored to fellowship. For such is the very nature of grace. Verses 6-8:

> 6 **Sufficient to such a man is this punishment, which was inflicted of [by] many.**
>
> 7 **So that contrariwise [However] ye ought rather to forgive him, and comfort him, lest perhaps such a one should be swallowed up with overmuch [overwhelming] sorrow.**
>
> 8 **Wherefore I beseech you that ye would confirm your love toward him.**

His punishment is enough for any man. Paul uses this as an example. Grace is *undeserved kindness* or *unmerited favor*. It is not earned and, in fact, is quite the opposite. For while we were yet sinners, still in our sinful and underserving condition, Christ died for us! (*cf.* Rom. 5:8.)

In the following verse, the word *proof* means *the results of trying or testing something to know its outcome*. Paul wants to ascertain some unknown quality or truth by an experiment or a test. Verses 9-11:

> 9 **For to this end [purpose] also did I write, that I might know the proof of you, whether ye be obedient in all things.**

> 10 **To whom ye forgive any thing, I forgive also: for if I forgave any thing, to whom I forgave it, for your sakes forgave I it in the person of Christ;**

> 11 **Lest Satan should get an advantage of us: for we are not ignorant of his devices.**

The proof is in their ability to forgive others. Discipline may solve a problem, but unforgiveness could give Satan a foothold within believers. Being like Christ and exercising grace, which is love and forgiveness, will prevent that possibility.

Timothy and Titus were both workers in the ministry with Paul. He had trained them and considered himself to be their father in the faith. Without modern communication, it was difficult to know the whereabouts of someone. Not knowing his location or state of wellbeing, Paul was concerned for Titus. They faced much opposition to the Gospel of Grace and were often in peril. Verses 12-13:

> **12 Furthermore, when I came to Troas to preach Christ's gospel, and a door was opened unto me of [by] the Lord,**

> **13 I had no rest in my spirit, because I found not Titus my brother: but taking my leave of them, I went from thence into Macedonia.**

Paul went to look for Titus. Macedonia is the region north of Greece and Aegean Sea. It would be about 5000 miles north of Corinth. Paul's fears are relieved once he was confident of Titus' safety.

Paul uses the word *savour* which was used in the Old Testament for something pleasing to God. This brings greater depth to the meaning. Let us take a moment and consider the word *savour* when it was first used in Genesis 8:20-21:

> **20 And Noah builded an altar unto the LORD; and took of every clean beast, and of every clean fowl, and offered burnt offerings on the altar.**

21 And the LORD smelled a sweet savour; and the LORD said in his heart . . .

This *savour* or sweet smell was pleasing and it moved
the LORD. Jesus used this word in the New Testament concerning the uselessness of salt. Luke 14:34:

34 Salt is good: but if the salt have lost
his [its] savour, wherewith shall it be
seasoned?

Later, Paul uses *savour* to describe God's delight with
Christ's sacrifice. Ephesians 5:1-2:

1 Be ye therefore followers of God, as
dear children; **2** And walk in love, <u>as
Christ also hath loved us, and hath
given himself for us an offering and a
sacrifice to God for a sweet-smelling savour.</u>

Now, we are ready to read 2 Corinthians 2:14:

14 Now thanks be unto God, which always causeth us to triumph in Christ,
and maketh manifest [known] the savour of his knowledge by [through] us
in every place.

Paul refers to making known the Gospel of Grace. Our victory or triumph, as believers, is *in Christ*. Our salvation is safe and secure *in Christ*. As such, we, being placed *in Christ*, carry the same sweet *savour* of Christ Himself. Verse 15:

> **15 For we are unto God a sweet savour of Christ, [both] in them that are saved, and in them that perish:**

Like the smell of Thanksgiving dinner cooking and its first taste, it reminds us of something. It is possible for a savour to remind each of us of something different. Verses 16:

> **16 To the one we are <u>the savour of death unto death</u>; and to the other <u>the savour of life unto life</u>. And who is sufficient for these things?**

To those who perish, it is a *savour* of death and, to those who are saved, it is the *savour* life.

Paul asks a question: Who is sufficient for these things? Our sufficiency is from God. We are *in Christ*. We can do all things through Christ who strengthens us. (*cf.* Phil. 4:13.) Christ alone is our sufficiency! He closes by mentioning the corruption of the Word of God. There are those who teach a different gospel. It is a worldly gospel corrupted by customs, traditions, and philosophies of men. Nevertheless, Paul and those who hold to the true gospel stand before God and speak the truth in Christ. Verse 17:

> 17 **For we are not as many, which corrupt the word of God: but as of sincerity, but as of God, in the sight of God speak we in Christ.**

4

2 Corinthians 3

In each believer, there is a testament, a statement, a story, or a letter upon which is written about Christ in us. This is the point that Paul makes in these next verses. He starts by asking a question similar to, "Should we all commend or boast about ourselves?" There is nothing we can boast about because Christ has done it all. We are His story written in us. When others see us, we are living testaments about our living Savior. 2 Corinthians 3:1-3:

> 1 **Do we begin again to commend ourselves? or need we, as some others, epistles of commendation to you, or letters of commendation from you?**
>
> 2 **Ye are our epistle written in our hearts, known and read of [by] all men:**

3 Forasmuch as ye are manifestly declared to be the epistle of Christ ministered by us, written not with ink, but with the Spirit of the living God; not in tables of stone, but in fleshy tables of the heart.

We have our letter or story about our life written upon our heart by our Lord Jesus Christ. We were bought and paid for by His Blood.

As we think about Christ's sufficiency, some may remember the words of this hymn penned in 1865 by Elvina M. Hall. She wrote, "Jesus paid it all, all to Him I owe." Like her, we can trust God that, in Christ, we have all that is necessary for our eternal salvation! Verses 4-6:

4 And such trust have we through Christ to God-ward: 5 Not that we are sufficient of ourselves to think any thing as of ourselves; but <u>our sufficiency is of God;</u>

6 Who also hath made us able ministers of the new testament; not of the letter [of the Law], but of the spirit: for the letter killeth, but the spirit giveth life.

He speaks of *the letter* referring to the Mosaic Law under which the Jews were obligated. This is "the letter of the Law" which condemns those who break it to death. For the Law has only the power to condemn and its punishment is death. However, the Spirit gives life. Each believer is given life through the Gospel of Grace and, therefore, each believer has a part in its ministry. Paul will outline this ministry in 2 Corinthians 5.

Moses received the Law directly from God while he was face to face with Him upon the mountain. Do you remember the stone tablets he received on top of Mount Sinai? The *ministration* or *purpose* of the Law was to condemn those who broke it. Its intent was to show Israel their ultimate need for a Savior. Verse 7:

> 7 **But if the ministration of death, written and engraven in stones, was glorious, so that the children of Israel could not stedfastly behold the face of Moses for [because of] the glory of [which shown on] his countenance [face]; which glory was to be done away [faded]:**

Paul compares the glory of the Law, given to Israel, with the glory of the Spirit. The glory of the Law will

Subside, but the glory of the Spirit is eternal. Verses 8-11:

> 8 How shall not the <u>ministration of the spirit</u> be rather [more] glorious?
>
> 9 For if the <u>ministration of condemnation</u> be glory, [how] much more doth the <u>ministration of righteousness</u> exceed in glory.
>
> 10 For even that which was made glorious had no glory in this respect, by reason of the glory that excelleth.
>
> 11 For if that which is done away was glorious, [how] much more [will] that which remaineth is glorious.

We need to stop for a moment to consider something not so obvious unless you are looking for it. Let us look again at the above verses and read it again from a different perspective. Let us consider replacing the word *ministration* with the word *dispensation* for they both mean the same thing.

Remember, a dispensation is a unique administration or *ministration* in which God rules His Creation. The phrases *ministration of the spirit* as well as

30

the *ministration of righteousness* both refer to the *Age of Grace!* However, the *dispensation of condemnation* refers to the *Age of Law* because the Law, given to Moses, can only condemn. How do we know this? Paul explains it in Romans 3:19-20:

> 19 **Now we know that what things soever the law saith, it saith to them who are under the law: that every mouth may be stopped, and <u>all the world may become guilty before God</u>.**
>
> 20 **Therefore <u>by the deeds of the law there shall no flesh be justified in his [God's] sight</u>: for by the law is the knowledge of sin.**

The purpose of the Law was to bring knowledge of sin. Sinful man has no defense or other choice than to turn to God for the solution.

We are told Moses received the Law while face to face with God. As a result, when returning to the people, his face beamed with a glorious radiance. He had to cover his face with a veil when he went before the people. You can find the story in Exodus 34:29-35. It is this glory to which Paul refers in 2 Corinthians 3:12-13:

12 Seeing then that we have such hope, we use great plainness of speech: 13 And not as Moses, which put a vail over his face, that the children of Israel could not stedfastly look to the end of that which is abolished:

The veil that Moses wore is the same veil which blinds the understanding of Israel today. This will remain in place until the appointed time. Verses 14-15:

14 But their minds were blinded: for until this day remaineth the same vail untaken away in the reading of the old testament; which vail is done away in Christ. 15 But <u>even unto this day, when Moses is read, the vail is upon their heart.</u>

I mentioned *their appointed time* above. Below, Paul makes this clear. When Israel turns to the Lord, the veil will be removed! Verse 16:

16 Nevertheless when it [Israel] shall turn to the Lord, the vail shall be taken away.

Paul now speaks about those who are saved by grace through faith. Each grace believer receives the

Holy Spirit as a downpayment. He guarantees the completion of their redemption. (*cf.* Eph. 1:13-14.) In the next verse, he speaks of the *liberty* of the believers. First, let us look at Paul's definition of the *liberty* of the believers. Romans 8:21:

> **21 Because the creature itself [those saved by grace] also shall be delivered from the bondage of corruption <u>into the glorious liberty of the children of God</u>.**

When we are saved, we receive the righteousness of Christ. We are adopted and made members of the household of God. We are God's children—children of light—and made co-heirs with Christ. This wonderful news is explained in depth in GraceWord's commentary on Ephesians. We must understand that all believers saved by grace are—*in Christ!*

Now, we can read 2 Corinthians 3:17:

> **17 Now the Lord is that Spirit: and <u>where the Spirit of the Lord is, there is liberty</u>.**

This *liberty* is freedom from the bondage or constraints of the Law. As grace believers we are no longer under the condemnation of the Law. Instead, we have the righteousness of Christ imparted to us at our salvation! The penalty for our sins — past, present, and future — has been paid in full. When believers are first told this, they challenged Paul with this question. Romans 6:15:

> 15 **What then? shall we sin, because we are not under the law, but under grace? God forbid.**

He follows this with his response. Verses 16-18:

> 16 **Know ye not, that to whom ye yield yourselves servants to obey, his servants ye are to whom ye obey; whether of sin unto death, or of obedience unto righteousness?**

> 17 **But God be thanked, that <u>ye were the servants of sin</u>, but ye have obeyed from the heart that form of doctrine which was delivered you.**

> 18 <u>**Being then made free from sin, ye became the servants of righteousness.**</u>

No longer being subject to the Law but under grace, Paul writes this in Romans 8:1:

> 1 **There is <u>therefore now no condemna-**</u>

tion to them which are in Christ Jesus, who walk not after the flesh, but after the Spirit.

There is nothing that can separate believers from God. For when God looks upon the believer, He does not see the righteousness of that believer, but He sees the righteousness of Christ in Whom the believer resides.

Those saved by grace through faith are seated with Him in heaven beside God the Father. Spiritually, we are *in Christ*. We are to await *His Calling*. Then, we will be changed into His image from glory to glory. Our glorified body will be like His. How wonderful is this! It is referred to as "the Blessed Hope" to which all believers must cling. Like the songwriter Dottie Rambo wrote, "We shall behold Him. Oh yes, we shall behold Him. Face to face my Savior and Lord!" Paul closes by speaking of our bodily redemption. 2 Corinthians 3:18:

> 18 **But we all, with open face beholding as in a glass [mirror] the glory of the Lord, are changed into the same image from glory to glory, even [that is to say] as by the Spirit of the Lord.**

5

2 Corinthians 4

In the previous chapter, we learned the glory of the Spirit will remain forever. Salvation of all grace believers is secured or guaranteed by the Spirit. Paul makes this clear in Ephesians 1:13-14:

> 13 In whom ye also trusted, after that ye heard the word of truth, the gospel of your salvation: in whom also <u>after that ye believed, ye were sealed with that holy Spirit of promise,</u>
>
> 14 Which is the earnest of our inheritance until the redemption of the purchased possession, unto the praise of his glory.

As believers, we have received liberty. We have been set free from the bondage of the Law through

Christ's fulfillment of the Law. Upon our salvation, we were given righteousness – not our own righteousness but His. Paul writes to the Galatians to warn them. Do not get caught up in the snare by mixing Law and grace. He refers to the Law as bondage. If any requirement is added to the simplicity of grace, then it diminishes the sufficiency of Christ's work on the Cross! Galatians 5:1:

> 1 **Stand fast** therefore **in the liberty wherewith Christ hath made us free,** and **be not entangled** again **with the yoke of bondage.**

We have Christ's righteousness. We received it as a gift when we believed in Christ's death, burial, and resurrection. Therefore, we can be confident that works play no part in our salvation.

We begin Chapter 4 with Paul drawing a conclusion from the previous chapter. 2 Corinthians 4:1:

> 1 **Therefore seeing we have this ministry, as we have received mercy [ourselves], we faint not;**

We do not give up because we know this is the truth of God. He will go into greater detail concerning this ministry later. Verse 2:

2 But have renounced the hidden things of dishonesty, not walking in craftiness, nor handling the word of God deceitfully; but by manifestation of [making known] the truth commending ourselves to every man's conscience in the sight of God.

As an example, we are to walk upright and blameless in the world. Like Paul, we must remain committed to the truth. Never deceitfully changing or altering the truth. Instead, we are to make it plain by rightly dividing the Word of Truth. (*cf.* 2 Tim. 2:15.)

Paul is speaking about a specific gospel. He received it from Christ concerning salvation by grace through faith without works. This message offers reconciliation to everyone who is lost and at enmity with God. Unfortunately, all mankind has free will and not everyone will accept His gracious offer. We are not to faint or grow weary. Our ministry is to only make the gospel known. Each individual will decide whether they will accept or reject the offer. Verses 3-4:

3 But if our gospel be hid, <u>it is hid to them that are lost</u>:

4 In whom <u>the god of this world hath</u>

**blinded the minds of them which be-
lieve not,** lest the light of the glorious
gospel of Christ, who is the image of
God, should shine unto them.

Contrary to what others teach, there is no sovereign
predestination of those who are saved. The enemy
clouds the minds of those who are lost. It is possible
for them to hear and, if they choose, believe. Therefore, faint not! Do not give up! Continue to persevere
in presenting the gospel of salvation.

We are not to be self-promoting. For us, it
should be all about Christ and not ourselves. The
preaching of the *Gospel of Grace* shines as a powerful
light into the darkness of unbelievers. It is this very
light which allows people to see the truth and make
their choice. Verses 5-6:

> 5 **For we preach not ourselves, but
> Christ Jesus the Lord; and ourselves [as]
> your servants for Jesus' sake.**

> 6 **For God, who commanded the light to
> shine out of darkness, hath shined in
> our hearts, to give the light of the
> knowledge of the glory of God in the
> face of Jesus Christ.**

Paul refers to this knowledge as a *treasure* saying that this *treasure* is stored in human bodies called *earthen vessels*. As believers, we are still made of clay. Therefore, we should not be proud or boastful in the ministry. Everything that is accomplished is by God's power and not our own. God has committed this ministry to weak vessels. Why? It is so that He may receive all the glory! Verse 7:

> 7 **But we have <u>this treasure in earthen vessels</u>, that the excellency of <u>the power may be of God, and not of us.</u>**

The Holy Spirit resides within each grace believer. We are to hold on tightly, by faith, to the promises God has made until the Rapture – the completion of our redemption. While we wait, all believers will suffer like Christ. Verses 8-12:

> 8 **We are troubled on every side, yet not distressed; we are perplexed, but not in despair; 9 Persecuted, but not forsaken; cast down, but not destroyed;**

> 10 **Always bearing about in the body the dying of the Lord Jesus, that the life also of Jesus might be made manifest in our body.**

11 For we which live are alway delivered unto death for Jesus' sake, that the life also of Jesus might be made manifest in our mortal flesh. **12** So then death worketh in us, but life in you.

Let us stop for a moment and take a look at verse 12. As grace believers, we will struggle in our present physical state. It is much like those who swim against the river's current. Opposition seems to be against us on every side. There is a reason for this. Paul explains it in Romans 8:16-18:

16 The Spirit itself beareth witness with our spirit, that <u>we are the children of God</u>:

17 And if children, then heirs; <u>heirs of God, and joint-heirs with Christ</u>; if so be that [if that is the case then] <u>we suffer with him</u>, that we may be also glorified together.

18 For I reckon that <u>the sufferings of this present time</u> are not worthy to be compared with <u>the glory which shall be revealed in us</u>.

The sufferings in our present body is part of the process of sanctification. It is detaching us or separating us from the world. Like Christ, we too are dying to the world. And, like Him, we will also receive everlasting life.

Christ will come for His own. At His Appearing, He will redeem or claim His purchased possession. (See Eph. 1:14.) Until then, as children of God, we are to be *holy* which means *separated unto God*. And, like Christ, we will struggle in our ministry against the opposition. It is for this reason, Paul wrote the following in Ephesians 6:12:

> 12 **For we <u>wrestle</u> [struggle] not against flesh and blood, but <u>against principalities</u>, <u>against powers</u>, <u>against the rulers of the darkness of this world</u>, <u>against spiritual wickedness in high places</u>.**

Paul's struggle against the opposition began when he received the Gospel of Grace from the Risen Lord. 1 Timothy 1:15-16:

> 15 **This is a faithful saying, and worthy of all acceptation, that Christ Jesus came into the world to save sinners; <u>of whom I [Paul] am chief</u>.**
>
> 16 **Howbeit for this cause I obtained**

mercy, that in me first Jesus Christ might shew forth all longsuffering, for a pattern to them which should hereafter believe on him to life everlasting.

Consider a dress-maker or a precision machinist. Each understands the importance of following a pattern or prototype. The word *longsuffering* means *to bear patiently with injuries or antagonism for a long time without being easily provoked.* Such is the case with Paul who was *longsuffering* as he followed Christ.

Paul was the first to hear and believe the *Gospel of Grace.* Having been the first to believe it, he was the first to proclaim this same gospel message to others. Each grace believer who, like him, choose to believe unto salvation must also proclaim this glorious *Gospel of Grace.* 2 Corinthians 4:13:

> 13 **We having [received] the same spirit of faith, according as it is written, I believed, and therefore have I spoken; we also believe, and therefore [must] speak;**

Consider the importance of this gospel message to the eternal destiny of all. Is it not selfish to keep this message to ourselves? It must be shared out of love and gratitude to the One Who saved us. It can be nothing else in that, by sharing it, we gain nothing ourselves. All the glory goes to Him Who is worthy! Verses 14-15:

> 14 **Knowing that he which raised up the Lord Jesus shall raise up us also by Jesus, and shall present us with you.**

> 15 **For all things are for your sakes, <u>that the abundant grace [shared] might through the thanksgiving of many redound to [result in] the glory of God.</u>**

For this purpose, ministry, or mission we must not faint although our earthly body perish. We are to rely completely upon God Who strengthens us day-by-day through His Spirit. Our afflictions and trials are but momentary when compared to the glory in eternity promised to us. Verses 16-17:

> 16 **For which cause we faint not; but though our outward man perish, yet the inward man is renewed day by day.**

> 17 **For our light affliction, which is but for a moment, worketh for us a far more exceeding and eternal weight of glory;**

The things which are seen by the human eye

are only *temporal* which means *for a time.* They are like the mist upon the waters which evaporates with the coming of the noonday sun. Those who have eyes of faith can see the *eternal* which are according to the promises of God. Therefore, grace believers, faint not but have faith! Verse 18:

> 18 **While we look not at <u>the things which are seen</u>, but at <u>the things which are not seen</u>: for the things which are seen are temporal; but <u>the things which are not seen are eternal</u>.**

6

2 Corinthians 5

A tabernacle can be a temporary dwelling like a tent. In the wilderness, God had the Jews construct a tabernacle as a temporary place for God's presence to reside. In the case of a human body, it is a temporary dwelling place for our spirit. Paul begins this chapter by comparing our earthly body with the one we will receive. He has promised us a glorified body like Christ's. 2 Corinthians 5:1:

> 1 **For we know that if our earthly house of this tabernacle were dissolved, we have a building of God, an house not made with hands, eternal in the heavens.**

Our new body we receive at the Rapture will be eternal as will our position *in Christ!*

We may groan in our earthly bodies, but we must hold onto the hope of the promise. What promise? The promise of our completed redemption – both of our spirit and our physical body. Verses 2-5:

> 2 For in this we groan, earnestly desiring to be clothed upon with our house which is from heaven: 3 If so be that being clothed we shall not be found naked.

> 4 For we that are in this tabernacle [temporary dwelling] do groan, being burdened: not for that we would be unclothed, but clothed upon, that mortality might be swallowed up of [by] life.

> 5 Now he that hath wrought [made] us for the selfsame thing [this very purpose] is God, who also hath given unto us the earnest of the Spirit.

Sometimes, repetition is the best way to learn. The word *earnest* is a very important word. We saw it in 2 Corinthians 1. *Earnest* is a legal word meaning *the deposit which secures the completion of the promised transaction.* In our case, the holy Spirit of Promise is the earnest that secures or guarantees the completion of our full redemption. (*cf.* Eph. 1:13-14.)

48

As we struggle under the weight of oppression and struggles, we can and must be confident of our future. Verses 6-8:

> 6 **Therefore we are always confident, knowing that, whilst we are at home in the [present] body, we are absent from the Lord:** 7 **(For we walk by faith, not by sight:)**

> 8 **We are confident, I say, and willing [eager] rather to be absent from the body, and to be present with the Lord.**

Most Christians who are confident in their bright future, would rather die and be present with their Lord. Believers, when they reach this point, realize they are only sojourners in a foreign land. This place is not their home. Friend, this is the process of sanctification. This is not something we do ourselves, but something that Someone else does for us. Here is what Paul says. Philippians 1:6:

> 6 **Being confident of this very thing, that he [God] which hath begun a good work in you [He] will perform it until the day of Jesus Christ:**

Like our salvation, our sanctification is being taken

care of for us. He will complete it by the Rapture.

In the next verses, it sounds as though our acceptance by Jesus Christ is contingent upon our meeting certain criteria. This is not the case at all. That interpretation would be inconsistent with the Gospel of Grace. For we know that we are already accepted in the Beloved. It is not because of what we have done, but because of what He has done for us. 2 Corinthians 5:9:

> 9 **Wherefore we labour, that, whether present or absent, we may be accepted of [by] him.**

Paul is speaking about himself and all who work for the furtherance of the gospel. We know that works play no part in our salvation – period. "There is therefore now no condemnation to them which are in Christ Jesus, who walk not after the flesh, but after the Spirit" (Rom. 8:1). Then, what is Paul saying here?

It has to do with the acceptability of our labors in the faith. Every believer is to *labor* concerning the Gospel of Grace. He is speaking about what artisans would call the *finished product* of their labors. Let us look back at 1 Corinthians 3:9-10:

9 For <u>we are labourers together with God</u>: ye are God's husbandry, ye are God's building.

10 <u>According to the grace of God</u> which is given unto me, as a wise master-builder, I [Paul] have laid the foundation, and another buildeth thereon. But <u>let every man take heed how he buildeth thereupon</u>.'

The foundation to which Paul refers is the message he received from Christ. He is speaking about the quality of our workmanship in this ministry. We continue with the above in verses 11-15:

11 For [any] other foundation can no man lay than that is laid, which is Jesus Christ. 12 Now if any man build upon this foundation gold, silver, precious stones, wood, hay, stubble;

13 <u>Every man's work shall be made manifest [revealed]</u>: for the day shall declare it, because it shall be revealed by fire; and the <u>fire shall try [test or judge] every man's work of what sort it is</u>.

14 If any man's work abide which he

hath built thereupon, he shall receive a reward. 15 <u>If any man's work shall be burned, he shall suffer loss [of reward]: but he himself shall be saved; yet so as by fire.</u>

If a man's work does not pass judgment, then his work will be lost even though he will be saved.

Again, this *labour* is the *work* of the gospel. The Judgment Seat of Christ is not the same as The Great White Throne. The latter is reserved for judgment of the unsaved. We know about the judgment of the unsaved and the terror it will bring. Therefore, out of gratitude to our Savior, we are to make known to others this same gospel by which we ourselves are saved! Now, we can return to 2 Corinthians 5:10-11:

10 **For we must all appear before the judgment seat of Christ; that every one may receive the things done in his body, according to that he hath done, whether it be good or bad.**

11 <u>**Knowing therefore the terror of the Lord, we persuade men;**</u> **but we are made manifest unto [known to] God; and I trust also [you] are made manifest [known] in your consciences.**

Our consciences should make us eager to do this for the One Who has done so much for us!

Paul makes no praise nor commends himself or his co-laborers. The Corinthians know the work that they do. There is no need to tell them again. Verse 12:

> **12 For we commend not ourselves again unto you, but give you occasion to glory on our behalf, that ye may have somewhat to answer them which glory in appearance, and not in heart.**

He gives them only a benchmark by which they can compare others. For there are those who work in the ministry for appearances sake only. They do it without sincerity of heart. Let the Corinthians answer them with this. Verses 13-14:

> **13 For whether we be beside ourselves, it is to God: or whether we be sober, it is for your cause.**

> **14 For the love of Christ constraineth us; because we thus judge, that if one died for all, then were all dead:**

> **15 And that he [Christ] died for all, <u>that they which live should not henceforth</u>**

live unto themselves, but unto him which died for them, and rose again.

He instructs them that from this point going forward they are to see things differently. Previously, in their flesh, they saw only Jews and non-Jews. Christ, while He was on earth, was a Jew. He came to fulfill the promises made to the fathers. (*cf.* Rom. 15:8.) But now, we are to no longer know Christ according to the flesh. For He, Christ, is no longer on earth. He is in heaven. Thus, we must see things according to the Spirit and not the flesh. Verse 16:

16 **Wherefore henceforth [going forward] know we no man after the flesh: yea, though we have known Christ after the flesh, yet now henceforth know we him no more.**

All grace believers are given the ministry of reconciliation. Paul explains that God's intent for the *Gospel of Grace* is to reconcile the lost unto Himself. This is the ministry to which we have been called. 2 Corinthians 5:17-19:

17 **Therefore <u>if any man be in Christ, he is a new creature</u>: old things are passed away; behold, all things are become new.**

18 And [now] all things are of God, who hath reconciled us to himself by Jesus Christ, and hath given to us the ministry of reconciliation;

19 To wit [knowing this], that God was in Christ, reconciling the world unto himself, not imputing their trespasses [sins] unto them; and hath committed unto us the word [gospel] of reconciliation.

It is our testimony! We know this is because we have experienced it ourselves. We have been reconciled to God. We who were once enemies of God have now been reconciled to Him through His Son. Romans 5:8-10:

8 But God commendeth his love toward us, in that, while we were yet sinners, Christ died for us. 9 Much more then, being now justified by his blood, we shall be saved from wrath through him.

10 For if, when we were enemies, we were reconciled to God by the death of his Son, much more, being reconciled, we shall be saved by his life.

Many churches show charity or love to the homeless and needy. They provide them with food and clothing, but never reconcile the lost to their heavenly Father. Do not confuse the ministry of the Kingdom Gospel with that of the Grace Gospel. Reconciling the lost is our primary directive. This is ministry!

Presently, there are only those who are *in Christ* and those who are not. There are only the saved and unsaved. Paul tells us that those who are *in Christ* are a new creation. 2 Corinthians 5:17:

> 17 **Therefore <u>if any man be in Christ, he is a new creature</u>: old things are passed away; behold, all things are become new.**

Friend, I hope you did not miss this truly wonderful news! Not only do we have eternal salvation, but we have also been "saved from wrath through him" (Rom. 8:9). Some question whether grace believers will go through the Tribulation. Here is your proof text. How can those who have the righteousness of His Son be judged and punished by the Father? They cannot. They are *in Christ!*

What is the ministry we have been given? It is *the ministry of reconciliation.* We are to allow God to use us. We are to work to reconcile the unsaved to a loving and gracious God. Verses 18-19:

> 18 **And all things are of God, <u>who hath reconciled us to himself</u> by Jesus Christ, <u>and hath given to us the ministry of reconciliation;</u>**

> 19 **To wit, that God was in Christ, reconciling the world unto himself, not imputing their trespasses unto them; <u>and hath committed unto us the word of reconciliation.</u>**

What is this *word of reconciliation?* It is the *Word of Truth.* It is the *Gospel of Grace.* This is God's purpose. We are told that, if we are "called according to His purpose," then "all things will work together for good." Romans 8:28:

> 28 **And we know that all things work together for good to them that love God, <u>to them who are the called according to his purpose.</u>**

Who are those called according to His purpose and what is God's singular purpose? God is restoring all Creation to Himself. God is reconciling the lost world to Himself through His Son. 1 Timothy 2:3-4:

3 For this is good and acceptable in the sight of God our Saviour; **4** Who will have [desires] all men to be saved, and to come unto the knowledge of the truth.

How has God chosen to do this? Verses 5-6:

5 For there is one God, and one mediator between God and men, the man Christ Jesus; **6** Who gave himself a ransom for all, to be testified in due time.

At the completion of God's restoration, Christ shall be revealed as God. He will receive His due honor. Isaiah 45:23:

23 I have sworn by myself, the word is gone out of my mouth in righteousness, and shall not return, That unto me every knee shall bow, every tongue shall swear.

Therefore, God has given each grace believer the *ministry of reconciliation*. That we, as if Christ Himself, are making known the truth of the Gospel of Grace to all men. Verse 20:

20 Now then we are ambassadors for

Christ, as though God did beseech you by us: we pray you in Christ's stead, be ye reconciled to God.

Again, why should we do this? While we were still sinners and helpless, God made His Son to be sin for us. He was crucified, dead, and buried. He rose again from the dead for our justification. Now, it is He Who is our righteousness. How can we not share this wonderful news? Verse 21:

21 **For he hath made him to be sin for us, who knew no sin; <u>that we might be made the righteousness of God in him.</u>**

7

2 Corinthians 6

As we pursue this *ministry of reconciliation*, we are not working alone. We are allowing the Holy Spirit to do God's work through us. 2 Corinthians 6:1:

> 1 **We then, as workers together with him [God], beseech you also that ye receive not the grace of God in vain.**

In the following verse, the word *succour* comes from the Latin verb *succurrere* which means *to run to someone's aid.* Verse 2:

> 2 **(For he saith, I have heard thee in a time accepted, and in the day of salvation have I succoured thee: behold, now is the accepted time; behold, now [presently] is <u>the day of salvation</u>.)**

Christ has appointed us to be *ambassadors*. When an ambassador speaks, it is as though the country were speaking. Therefore, when we speak, we are speaking on Christ's behalf as if Christ Himself was speaking. Since we represent Him, our actions and demeanor are important. We will be judged by others as Christ's representatives.

Paul teaches how we, as ambassadors, should act. Verses 3-6:

> 3 **Giving no offence [to anyone] in any thing, that the ministry be not blamed:** 4 **But in all things approving ourselves as the ministers of God, in much patience, in afflictions, in necessities, in distresses,**

> 5 **In stripes, in imprisonments, in tumults, in labours, in watchings, in fastings;** 6 **By pureness, by knowledge, by longsuffering, by kindness, by the Holy Ghost, by love unfeigned [not faked],**

He refers to the Scriptures as *the word of truth*. This is the only standard or authority by which we are to speak and act. Verses 7-10:

> 7 **By the word of truth, by the power of**

God, by the armour of righteousness on the right hand and on the left, 8 By honour and dishonour, by evil report and good report: as deceivers, and yet true;

9 As unknown, and yet well known; as dying, and, behold, we live; as chastened, and not killed; 10 As sorrowful, yet alway rejoicing; as poor, yet making many rich; as having nothing, and yet possessing all things.

This seems like a tall order. However, these are the outpourings of the love which Christ continues to show us. Remember, that while we were still sinners, Christ chose to die for us. (*cf.* Rom. 5:6-11.) With Christ as our example, should we not extend this same love and kindness towards others—both the saved and unsaved alike?

In the following verses, the word *bowels* is used. In its plural form it means *the innermost parts of someone* and represents *the individual's seat of emotions: pity, kindness, tenderness and compassion.* Verses 11-13:

11 O ye Corinthians, our mouth is open unto you, our heart is enlarged. 12 Ye are

**not straitened in us, but ye are strait-
ened in your own bowels.**

**13 Now for a recompence in the same, (I
speak as unto my children,) be ye also
enlarged.**

Paul writes to them "as unto my children" (v. 13).
The word *straitened* is a verb meaning *to be convicted
or resolved as in a singular purpose.* The word *recom-
pense* means *to repay, compensate, or make restitution.*
We will never be able to *repay* God for His grace, but
we can *be resolved* to show our gratitude by being
committed to the gospel. Therefore, let our hearts be
enlarged so they overflow with love for those who are
not reconciled to God.

Anything that takes away our attention from
this ministry must be avoided. This includes partner-
ing with non-believers. Paul knows the assembly at
Corinth very well. Let me put it this way. Many of
the believers there could wear a tee shirt saying,
"Wild Child!" Yet, they are saved! Being saved, they
are children of God and adopted into His family.
However, they are far from being separated from the
world. Verses 14-16:

**14 Be ye not unequally yoked together
with unbelievers: for what fellowship**

hath righteousness with unrighteousness? and what communion hath light with darkness?

15 And what concord [in common] hath Christ with Belial? or what part hath he that believeth with an infidel?

16 And what agreement hath the temple of God with idols? for ye are the temple of the living God; as God hath said, I will dwell in them, and walk in them; and I will be their God, and they shall be my people.

Remember, the process of sanctification is separating the believer from the world. We are being fitted for heaven where we will forever be the sons and daughters of God Almighty. Verses 17-18:

17 Wherefore come out from among them, and <u>be ye separate</u>, saith the Lord, and touch not the unclean thing; and <u>I will receive you,</u> 18 <u>And will be a Father unto you, and ye shall be my sons and daughters</u>, saith the Lord Almighty.

8

2 Corinthians 7

This is a continuation of the last chapter in which Paul calls all believers to be worthy of their calling. 2 Corinthians 7:1:

> **1 Having therefore these promiscs, dearly beloved, let us cleanse ourselves from all filthiness of the flesh and spirit, perfecting holiness in the fear of [respect for] God.**

Whether they receive Paul in person or by the words he writes them, they know he cares for their well-being and success in the faith. He and his fellow workers set an example for them. Verse 2:

> **2 Receive us; we have wronged no man, we have corrupted no man, we have defrauded no man.**

Not writing words of condemnation, although he perhaps should, he shows nothing but words of concern and love for them. Verse 3:

> 3 I speak not this to condemn you: for I have said before, that ye are in our hearts to die and live with you.

Paul knows that after death, they will be together in the presence of God for eternity. Even in tribulation which they all suffer, he still glories in them and is filled with comfort and joy. Verse 4:

> 4 Great is my boldness of speech toward you, great is my glorying of you: I am filled with comfort, I am exceeding joyful in all our tribulation.

When they came to Macedonia, there was great affliction. During this time, Titus came with news concerning the Corinthians. It brought relief to Paul knowing their concern for him. Verses 5-7:

> 5 For, when we were come into Macedonia, our flesh had no rest, but we were troubled on every side; without [outside] were fightings, within were fears.

> 6 Nevertheless God, that comforteth

those that are cast down, comforted us by the coming of Titus;

7 And not by his coming only, but by the consolation wherewith he was comforted in you, when he told us [about] your earnest desire, your mourning, your fervent mind toward me; so that I rejoiced the more.

Paul does not regret the content of his previous letter. It caused them some sorrow, but he knew it would be only temporary. All in all, his intent was never to injure them. His previous letter had served its intended purpose and brought some to stop and change their ways. Verses 8-9:

8 For though I made you sorry with a letter, I do not repent, though I did repent: for I perceive that the same epistle hath made you sorry, though it were but for a season.

9 Now I rejoice, not that ye were made sorry, but that ye sorrowed to repentance: for ye were made sorry after a godly manner, that ye might receive damage [injury] by us in nothing.

Only believers can experience genuine sorrow because it is caused by the Holy Spirit. Paul is not speaking about repentance for salvation. Instead, repentance causes us to stop what we are doing and change. Sorrow causes the believer to separate from worldliness. This is *sanctification.* This is separation from the world that causes death! Verse 10:

> 10 **For godly sorrow worketh repentance to salvation not to be repented of: but the sorrow of the world worketh death.**

In the next verse, the word *carefulness* means *being full of care.* In other words, it means *full of anxiety!* Look at the change of emotions. Verse 11:

> 11 **For behold this selfsame [very] thing, that ye sorrowed after a godly sort, what carefulness [anxiety] it wrought [caused] in you, yea, what clearing of yourselves, yea, what indignation, yea, what fear, yea, what vehement desire, yea, what zeal, yea, what revenge! In all things ye have approved yourselves to be clear in this matter.**

The report which Paul received concerning these matters had proved to him their desire to be acceptable to God.

Paul refers to a matter he discussed in his last letter. It concerned the unacceptable behavior of a certain member in the assembly. 1 Corinthians 5:1-2:

> 1 **It is reported commonly that there is fornication among you, and such fornication as is not so much as named among the Gentiles, that one should have his father's wife.**

> 2 **And ye are puffed up, and have not rather mourned, that he that hath done this deed might be taken away [removed] from among you.**

Referring to this matter, he writes in 2 Corinthians 7:12:

> 12 **Wherefore, though I wrote unto you, I did it not for his cause that had done the wrong, nor for his cause that suffered wrong, but that our care for you in the sight of God might appear unto you.**

It was his care for them that caused him to write them. It was not so much the sin itself, but their willingness to overlook it within the assembly.

The good news from Titus concerning their assembly refreshed Paul and he boasts about them. Here, the word *boast* means *to speak with laudable pride* concerning them. Verse 13-14:

> 13 **Therefore we were comforted in your comfort: yea, and exceedingly the more joyed we for the joy of Titus, because his spirit was refreshed by you all.**

> 14 **For if I have boasted any thing to him of you, I am not ashamed; but as we spake all things to you in truth, even so our boasting, which I made before Titus, is found a truth.**

Paul was filled with joy for them. Titus' memories of them and their reception of him causes him to have great love towards them. He remembers them and their deep desire to be obedient to the Word of God. Verse 15:

> 15 **And his [Titus'] inward affection is more abundant toward you, whilst he remembereth the obedience of you all, how with fear and trembling ye received him.**

With all of Paul's sufferings and rejection, this was a source of rejoicing. This news was consolation to him. He is their father in the faith and it brought him tremendous joy. He tells them that his confidence in them has been renewed. Verse 16:

> 16 I rejoice therefore that I have confidence in you in all things.

9

2 Corinthians 8

The believers in Corinth were financially better off than most other assemblies. Presently, there was no life-threatening event to bring people to God. There is an old saying, "There are no atheists in foxholes" as the soldiers on the front line are close to the possibility of death. So, these Corinthians were prosperous and wanting for nothing. This may have been the cause of their moral indifference.

Paul begins by discussing the generosity of the assemblies in Macedonia, the region north of Greece. 2 Corinthians 8:1-2:

> 1 **Moreover [Additionally], brethren, we do you to wit [make you aware] of the grace of God bestowed on the churches of Macedonia;**

2 How that in a great trial of affliction the abundance of their joy and their deep poverty abounded unto the riches of their liberality.

The assemblies in Macedonia were suffering from deep poverty and, yet, they had great joy. Out of their meager possessions, they showed their generosity by providing a financial support for Paul. They insisted he take their gift which was given out of their *liberality* or *generosity*. That is truly a free will offering.

They were willing to share out of their poverty in order to be part of the ministry. This is the ministry all believers are to share. Verses 3-4:

3 For to their power [ability], I bear record, yea, and beyond their power [ability] they were willing of themselves;

4 Praying [Asking] us with much intreaty that we would receive the gift, and take upon us the fellowship of the ministering to the saints.

The assemblies in Macedonia had received their salvation from the Lord. He saved them by His grace through their faith in His finished work. Then, because of this grace so freely given, they earnestly sought to partake in this ministry.

Their desire to be part of this is the outpouring of the Holy Spirit. These believers wanted to be part of the *ministry of reconciliation*. Verse 5:

> 5 **And this they did, not as we hoped, but [they] first gave their own selves to the Lord [by believing], and [then gave] unto us by the will of God.**

Paul did not solicit their support. The Spirit stirred their hearts and they implored Paul to allow them to be partners with him.

Paul had sent Titus to the Corinthians to strengthen their faith. It is his hope that as they would *abound in everything*. Verses 6-7:

> 6 **Insomuch that we desired Titus, that as he had begun, so he would also fin-ish in you the same grace also.**
>
> 7 **Therefore, as ye abound in every thing, in faith, and utterance, and knowledge, and in all diligence, and in your love to us, see that ye [do] also.**

We cannot forget that, in spite of his love for the believers, Paul still remains their apostle. He is not ordering or commanding them. Instead he is teaching them a valuable lesson. Verse 8:

> 8 **I speak not by commandment, but by occasion of the forwardness of others, and to prove the sincerity of your love.**

He wants them to understand the very essence of *grace.* How can he see them *abound in this grace* — generosity — unless they fully understand it like those in Macedonia? Verse 9:

> 9 **For <u>ye know the grace of our Lord Jesus Christ</u>, that, though <u>he was rich</u>, yet for your sakes <u>he became poor</u>, that ye through his poverty might be rich.**

Let all of us think about the riches of Christ. Think about what He gave up in order to accomplish what He did on our behalf. Philippians 2:5-8:

> 5 **Let this mind be in you, which was also in Christ Jesus: 6 Who, <u>being in the form of God</u>, thought it not robbery to be equal with God:**
>
> 7 **But <u>made himself of no reputation</u>,**

**and <u>took upon him the form of a serv-</u>
<u>ant</u>, and was <u>made in the likeness of</u>
<u>men</u>:**

8 And being found in fashion as a man,
<u>he humbled himself, and became obe-</u>
<u>dient unto death, even the death of the</u>
<u>cross</u>.

Christ, being God, gave up everything in order to die on the Cross for mankind. Paul wanted the Corinthians to remember this fact. It was Christ Who gave them salvation through *grace. Grace* is a *gift of God.* Their response should be a desire to share this *gift of God* with others.

We must pause for a moment to consider an historical event. Following Christ's death, the Twelve continued to minister to the Kingdom Believers. These believers were the Jews who were waiting for the Kingdom promised by their Messiah. Do you remember Jesus proclaiming the Kingdom of God is "at hand" in the gospels? (*cf.* Mt. 3:2, 4:17, 10:7; Mk 1:15; Lk. 2131.) Luke records the following at the beginning of Acts. Acts 2:41-44:

41 Then they that gladly received his
word were baptized: and the same day
there were added unto them about three

thousand souls. 42 And they continued stedfastly in the apostles' doctrine and fellowship, and in breaking of bread, and in prayers.

43 And fear came upon every soul: and many wonders and signs were done by the apostles.

44 <u>And all that believed were together, and had all things common; 45 And sold their possessions and goods, and parted them to all men, as every man had need.</u>

Having sold all their possessions and shared the proceeds, these Jewish believers were left destitute when the Kingdom was delayed.

In the meeting between Paul and the Twelve, an agreement was made concerning the two gospel messages and their respective recipients. However, they asked Paul to remember the need of the Jewish believers. Galatians 2:9-10:

9 And when James, Cephas, and John, who seemed to be pillars, perceived the grace that was given unto me, they gave to me and Barnabas the right hands of fellowship; that we should go unto the

heathen, and they unto the circumcision.

10 Only they would [asked] that we should remember the poor; the same which I also was forward [willing] to do.

Paul approached all the grace assemblies. He asked for a collection to be made for the benefit of these Kingdom believers. He would deliver this collection for these saints to Jerusalem in person.

At Paul's first request, the Corinthians were eager to contribute. He reminds them by saying now is the time to do their part. The following verses have to do with motivating them to complete their promise. 2 Corinthians 8:10-11:

> **10 And herein I give my advice: for this is expedient for you, who have begun before, not only to do, but also to be forward a year ago.**

> **11 Now therefore perform the doing of it; that as there was a readiness to will, so there may be a performance also out of that which ye have.**

They are to give according to what each man has and not what he does not. Verse 12:

> 12 **For if there be first a willing mind, it is accepted according to that [what] a man hath, and not according to that [what] he hath not.**

Each of us, like the Corinthians, should give from a willingness of the heart. Paul does not want to burden anyone. Verse 13:

> 13 **For I mean not that other men be eased, and ye burdened:**

Paul teaches a lesson in giving. Out of each believer's abundance should the gift be given. This gift will be received by those who are in need. Out of God's abundance He gave His Son Jesus Christ for the unsaved. Christ became the hope for those who had no hope. Verses 14-15:

> 14 **But by an equality, that now at this time your abundance may be a supply for their want, that their abundance also may be a supply for your want: that there may be equality:**

> 15 **As it is written, He that had gathered**

much had nothing over; and he that had gathered little had no lack.

Paul calls this *equality.* The Kingdom believers had sold everything and distributed it among those in need. When things turned bad, they were destitute. He asks grace believers to share from their abundance. They give to those who lack so that the joy of those who receive might be shared with those who give. This is *equality.*

Titus cared greatly for the assembly at Corinth. He was coming to them of his own choice having his heart stirred by the Spirit. Another brother who is unnamed yet known by the Corinthians is being sent as well. When the collection for the Jerusalem believers is brought to them, this man will be a delegate. Verses 16-19:

> 16 **But thanks be to God, which put the same earnest care into the heart of Titus for you.** 17 **For indeed he accepted the exhortation; but being more forward [willing], of his own accord he went unto you.**

> 18 **And we have sent with him the brother, whose praise is in the gospel throughout all the churches;**

19 And not that only, but who was also chosen of [by] the [other] churches to travel with us with this grace [gift], which is administered by us to the glory of the same Lord, and declaration [evidence] of your ready [willingness of] mind:

Many theologians believe the unnamed person is the beloved doctor Luke who often traveled with Paul.

Paul does not want to be accused of misappropriation. For this will be a sizeable donation taken to Jerusalem. All things must be open and above board. Therefore, delegates will be chosen by each assembly. Verses 20-21:

20 Avoiding this, that no man should blame us in this abundance which is administered by us: **21** Providing for honest things, not only in the sight of the Lord, but also in the sight of men.

He is confident enough that this unnamed brother needs no introduction. He has proven himself many times to be trustworthy. Verse 22:

22 And we have sent with them our brother, whom we have oftentimes

proved diligent in many things, but now much more diligent, upon the great confidence which I have in you.

Should one question Titus' trustworthiness as a delegate, Paul vouches for him personally in verse 23:

23 **Whether any do enquire of Titus, he is my partner and fellow-helper concerning you: or our brethren be enquired of, they are the messengers of the churches, and the glory of Christ.**

To these two delegates, Paul directs the Corinthian believers to show their love and generosity. This will be evidence of their love and proof that Paul's boasting of them was not in vain. Verse 24:

24 **Wherefore shew ye to them, and before the churches, the proof of your love, and of our boasting on your behalf.**

10

2 Corinthians 9

In the previous chapter, Paul seeks to motivate the Corinthians to make good on their pledge towards the collection from all the assemblies. Now, he wants to encourage them. 2 Corinthians 9:1-2:

1 For as touching [concerning] the ministering to the saints, it is superfluous [beyond need] for me to write to you:

2 For I know the forwardness [eagerness] of your mind, for which I boast of [about] you to them of Macedonia, that Achaia was ready a year ago; and your zeal hath provoked [moved] very many.

Some assemblies, like those in Achaia, were ready a year ago. However, it was the zeal of the Corinthians that moved the other assemblies to action.

When Paul's delegates arrive at Corinth, he would like them to be ready. Verses 3-5:

> 3 Yet have I sent the brethren, lest our boasting of you should be in vain in this behalf; that, as I said, ye may be ready:

> 4 Lest haply [by chance] if they of Macedonia come with me, and find you unprepared, we (that we say not, ye) should be ashamed in this same confident boasting.

> 5 Therefore I thought it necessary to exhort the brethren, [by this letter] that they would go before unto you, and make up beforehand your bounty, whereof ye had notice before, that the same might be ready, as a matter of bounty, and not as of covetousness.

Paul is giving them advanced notice. His intent is to collect their contribution when the party from Macedonia comes to them. They should be ready as a matter of generosity and not of stinginess.

How should one contribute to the work of the ministry? Verses 6-7:

6 But this I say, He which soweth sparingly shall reap also sparingly; and he which soweth bountifully shall reap also bountifully.

7 Every man according as he purposeth [determines] in his heart, so let him give; not grudgingly, or of necessity: for God loveth a cheerful giver.

He discusses sowing and reaping. This is giving and getting in return like a farmer who plants expecting a harvest which is his reward. Unlike the health and wealth preachers, I do not believe he is speaking of earthly rewards. We are planting spiritually and, therefore, should expect spiritual rewards. Paul speaks of rewards given to those who labor in the ministry. 1 Corinthians 3:7-8:

7 So then neither is he that planteth any thing, neither he that watereth; but [it is] God that giveth the increase.

8 Now he that planteth and he that watereth are one: and <u>every man shall receive his own reward according to his own labour.</u>

We are to give generously and cheerfully with

a willing heart. God provides. We are the laborers. Verse 8:

> 8 And God is able to make all grace abound toward you; that ye, always having [been given] all sufficiency in all things, may abound to every good work:

We may wonder if those more worthy receive more than those less worthy. However, it is for God to determine the appropriate gifts so that in all things God may receive the praise. Look at Ephesians 4:7:

> 7 But <u>unto every one of us is given grace according to the measure of the gift of Christ</u>.

Paul continues in 2 Corinthians 9:9-10:

> 9 (As it is written, He hath dispersed abroad; he hath given to the poor: his righteousness remaineth for ever.

> 10 Now he that ministereth seed to the sower both minister bread for your food, and multiply your seed sown, and increase the fruits of your righteousness;)

Ultimately, it is the One who provides the seed who provides all. One person may plant the seed, another tend to or water it. Another may harvest it and another makes bread from the grain. It is all about the One Who provides the seed. Paul quotes from Psalms 112:9:

> 9 **He [God] hath dispersed, he [God] hath given to the poor; his [God's] righteousness endureth for ever; his [God's] horn shall be exalted with honour.**

Do you see that word *horn?* It refers to *His Son* or offspring. His *horn* is the Lord Jesus Christ and He shall be exalted with honor!

God has never been stingy with His grace and mercy. Paul wants the Corinthians to overflow *in everything to all bountifulness!* Verse 11:

> 11 **Being enriched in every thing to all bountifulness, which causeth through us thanksgiving to God.**

This overflowing of abundance produces a spilling over of love from within the believers. Not only does this supply others who are in need, it also causes an abundant of thanksgiving to God. Verse 12:

12 For the administration of this service not only supplieth the want of the saints, but is abundant also by many thanksgivings unto God;

In the next verse, Paul uses the word *experiment* to mean *this new act or procedure*. Some of the assemblies provided for Paul's personal financial needs, this would be the first general collection made among the grace assemblies. Verse 13:

13 Whiles by the experiment of this ministration they glorify God for your professed subjection unto the gospel of Christ, and for your liberal distribution unto them, and unto all men;

Their act of giving this contribution to the Kingdom saints glorifies God for two reasons. First, it is evidence of the Corinthian's *subjection unto the gospel of Christ.* They had accepted the work of Christ's death, burial, and resurrection. They demonstrate this grace to others who belong to Him. Second, their *liberal* or *generous* contributions are evidence of their gratitude.

Upon receipt of these donations or gifts, the recipients in Jerusalem will pray for them and thank God for their generosity. This is the gratitude all be-

lievers should have towards God due to His grace –
the gift of God. Verse 14:

> 14 **And by their prayer for you, which
> long after you for the exceeding grace of
> God in you.** 15 **Thanks be unto God for
> his unspeakable gift.**

11

2 Corinthians 10

Paul writes to the Corinthians with boldness before he comes to them in person. He must chastise them, but he wants to do it with the *meekness and gentleness of Christ*. He uses the word *bold* to mean *stern or direct in his demeanor*. As their apostle, he must teach them. 2 Corinthians 10:1:

> 1 **Now I Paul myself beseech you by the meekness and gentleness of Christ, who in presence am base [lowly] among you, but being absent am bold toward you:**

When Paul is present with them in Corinth, he is lowly like a servant. Now, he writes to them with boldness and they need to listen.

He implores them that, when he comes to them in person, his boldness will no longer be needed. Verse 2:

2 But I beseech you, that I may not be bold when I am present with that confidence, wherewith I think to be bold against some, which think of us as if we walked according to the flesh.

Believers may be saved by grace, but some will continue to walk according to the flesh. This means that they see and do things from a human or worldly perspective.

Paul is feeding them meat here. They need to change their perspective. Now, being saved from the carnal or fleshly world, they must see things from a spiritual perspective! Verses 3-4:

3 For though we walk in the flesh, we do not war after the flesh: 4 (For the weapons of our warfare are not carnal, but mighty through God to the pulling down of strong holds;)

Yes, our present state is in the flesh as we await the Rapture. However, Paul wants us to see that we do not war against flesh and blood. Our battles are not against people since our battles are spiritual in nature. Ephesians 6:12:

> 12 **For we wrestle not against flesh and blood, but against principalities, against powers, against the rulers of the darkness of this world, against spiritual wickedness in high places.**

These battles can only be seen through eyes of faith. We must change our perspective. All believers will experience the effects of these spiritual battles. In the end, God will restore Creation completely. He will exalt the Lord Jesus Christ over everything—both in heaven and on earth. However, until then, our adversaries are in the spiritual realm. They fight against God and all that belong to Him. That includes us—His adopted children. 2 Corinthians 10: 5:

> 5 **Casting down imaginations [false beliefs], and every high thing that exalteth itself against the knowledge of God, and bringing into captivity every thought to the obedience of Christ;**

In the next verse, Paul refers to the Tribulation which is the wrath of God to come. During the Age of Grace, God is patiently waiting offering amnesty and grace to all. However, He will release His righteous judgment upon the wicked. Seven years remain for the Age of Law according to Daniel's prophecy. The Rapture will conclude the Age of Grace and signal the beginning of the Tribulation. Verse 6:

> 6 **And [God] having in a readiness to revenge all disobedience, <u>when [once] your obedience is fulfilled</u>.**

Read this underlined portion again. God is ready to revenge or judge the disobedient—those who have rejected Him. Wait! When will this happen? We must remember that Paul is writing to those saved by grace—grace believers. That is us! He tells the Corinthians that this revenge will take place once their *obedience is fulfilled!*

Do not struggle with this. We have been saved by what Christ has already done for us, right? Earlier, I told you that it is He "which hath begun a good work in you will perform it until the day of Jesus Christ" (Phil. 1:6). Friend, there is more good news! Our *sanctification,* which was begun when we believed, will be completed by Christ! The words *the day of Jesus Christ* refer specifically to the day of the Rapture. Christ appears in the air and calls His own to Himself. This will conclude the Age of Grace and the Age of Law will resume. There are seven years still remaining. This will be a period of testing for true Israel. Those who rebel against God and reject Him will suffer the consequences.

It would be impossible for God to include those who are saved by grace! Why? If He did, then He would be judging His Own Son Who is righteous. We are *in Christ*. Look at 2 Corinthians 1:21:

> 21 Now <u>he [God] which stablisheth us</u> with <u>you in Christ</u>, and hath anointed us, is God;

It is God Who establishes us *in Christ*. Spiritually, we are *in Christ*. Grace believers only await their bodily redemption. While we are here, we will suffer like Christ. He also suffered during His earthly ministry. There is an important reason for this. It is our *sanctification!* This is what separates grace believers from the world. Look at the last verse above and notice that God *has anointed us*. He has already done this. To *anoint* means *to declare or set apart as sacred*. It was the act of *sanctification!* The word *when* always refers to a time. At the time when this process is complete, grace believers will be called up to Him at the Rapture. This will be the end of the Age of Grace.

We tend to look at things from the outside. This is a worldly perspective. 2 Corinthians 10:7:

7 Do ye look on things after the outward appearance? If any man trust to himself that he is Christ's, let him of himself think this again, that, as he is Christ's, even so are we Christ's.

Each believer belongs to Christ as does Paul and the others who are ministers of grace. For in Christ there is no distinction between believers. (*cf.* Rom. 3:22.) All believers are the same. As the Apostle to the Gentiles, Paul was given the care of these believers. Verses 8-11:

8 For though I should boast somewhat more of our authority, which the Lord hath given us for [your] edification, and not for your destruction, I should not be ashamed:

9 That I may not seem as if I would terrify you by letters. 10 For [some say] his letters, say they, are weighty and powerful; but his bodily presence is weak, and his speech contemptible.

11 Let such an one think this, that, such as we are in word by letters when we are absent, such will we be also in deed when we are present.

Paul seeks only to benefit them. The purpose of his instruction is for their spiritual welfare whether it be by letter or in person.

Paul compares himself and those who minister with him to the others who commend or promote themselves. He says this is foolishness. These others strive amongst themselves comparing themselves one to another. Verse 12:

> 12 **For we dare not make ourselves of the number [these others], or compare ourselves with some that commend themselves: but they [who are] measuring themselves by themselves, and comparing themselves among themselves, are not wise.**

Those who are true ministers of grace know that it is all about God. We only serve to carry out His work.

It is God Who sets the limits just as He established the boundaries of the sea. (*cf.* Prov. 8:29.) We see an example of God establishing limits in Paul's own ministry. At one point, he was forbidden by the Spirit to preach the word in Asia. (*cf.* Acts 16:6.). It was clear to Paul that God set the *measure*. Here, the word *measure* means *the limit or quantity; the determination of the extent or boundary.* Verse 13:

13 But we will not boast of things without our measure, <u>but according to the measure of the rule which God hath distributed to us</u>, a measure to reach even unto you.

We must know the *measure* God has ordained for us and not go beyond the limits God established. Instead, in faith, we must trust God and leave it to Him to determine.

This actually takes a lot of the stress off the believer. When working in the ministry of grace, we must accept and stay within God's *measure*. In our fleshly minds, we strive to reach beyond the measure that God has *given to us*. Verses 14-15:

14 For we stretch not ourselves beyond our measure, as though we reached not unto you: for we are come as far as to you also in preaching the gospel of Christ:

15 Not boasting of things without [outside] our measure, that is, of other men's labours; but having hope, when your faith is increased, that we shall be enlarged [encouraged] by you according to our rule abundantly,

Paul speaks about his own ministry. They have reached as far as Corinth preaching the gospel of grace. He is encouraged by the spiritual growth and wellbeing of all grace believers. With all the trials and tribulations he faces, their prospering in the faith is a source of joy for him. He tells them that *when your faith is increased* he hopes God will greatly increase his limit or measure to reach more people.

Paul hopes to carry the message of the gospel beyond the regions of Corinth. This will happen only if God chooses to extend their *measure.* Verse 16:

> 16 **To preach the gospel in the regions beyond you, and not to boast in another man's line of things made ready to our hand.**

If any are to glory, then let them glory in the Lord. It is not about commending oneself that counts. It makes no sense to boast of one's accomplishments in *the ministry of reconciliation.* The Lord will judge the quality of workmanship. Therefore, let it be the Lord Who commends us. Verses 17-18:

> 17 **But he that glorieth, let him glory in the Lord. 18 For not he that commendeth himself is approved, but whom the Lord commendeth.**

12

2 Corinthians 11

We might forget that Paul is human. He deals with the same emotions we all do. At the beginning of this chapter, he refers to these emotions as his *folly* or *foolishness*. This may be his own insecurities or a personal lack of good judgment. All writers of Scripture are human with human frailties. However, this did not prevent God from using them to establish His Word. Paul asks the reader to bear with him as he explains. 2 Corinthians 11:1:

> 1 **[I] Would [hope] to God ye could bear with me a little in my folly: and indeed [that you do] bear with me.**

He uses an analogy to compare the believer's faithfulness to Christ as one's fidelity to a spouse. Here, the Lord Jesus Christ would be the husband.

The word *jealous* means *suspiciously vigilant or anxiously careful*. Paul is concerned they have lost their first love. They initially received the *Gospel of Grace* with such passion and eagerness as a young man would his spouse. He desires that they retain what they were taught and remain pure or unaffected by the teachings of others. Verse 2:

> 2 **For I am jealous over you with godly jealousy: for I have espoused you to one husband, that I may present you as a chaste virgin to Christ.**

The word *espoused* would be married in which the two share in intimate and personal relationship. This is how the believer's bond or connection with Christ should always be.

There are many outside influences within the Corinthian assembly. The Judaizers taught that grace alone was not sufficient without the Law. There were also Greek philosophers teaching the knowledge of man. Both of these were striving to seduce the believers away from their first love. They challenged the doctrines and even contested the validity of Paul's apostleship. We must not forget this. The powers, principalities, and rulers of darkness are always in spiritual warfare with the saints. Verse 3:

3 But I fear, lest by any means, as the serpent beguiled Eve through his subtilty, so your minds should be corrupted from the simplicity that is in Christ.

The Gospel of Grace is the simple truth. Salvation comes by believing in the finished work of Christ's death, burial, and resurrection. Compare this to the simplicity of God's instructions to Adam and Eve. The word *serpent* above refers to *Satan* who appeared as a *serpent* in the Garden of Eden. Satan is called *the father of lies* and he hates the truth of God. (*cf.* Jn 8:44.) Satan does not rest and continually seeks to corrupt God's truth. The Word of God is constantly under attack by God's enemy.

These non-believers have come into their assembly. They corrupted the truth and taught error. Verse 4:

4 For if he that cometh preacheth another Jesus, whom we have not preached, or if ye receive another spirit, which ye have not received, or another gospel, which ye have not accepted, ye might well bear with him.

I must admit the Paul's use of the words *bear with* twice in the chapter was puzzling. At first, he asks them to *bear with me* and, later, to *bear with him*. The latter being someone who is corrupting the truth. Then, I thought, that is the point. To *bear with* is similar *to put up with* or *tolerate* something. Is this not what the Corinthians were doing with these corrupters in their midst? Should they not have shown them to the door by the scruff of the neck and the seat of their pants?

They were challenging Paul's apostleship by pointing out that he was not one of the Twelve. Neither was he with the Messiah during His earthly ministry. All of this is true. However, God had set Paul apart for a singular reason. Ananias was told by God that, ". . . he is a chosen vessel unto me, to bear my name before the Gentiles, and kings, and the children of Israel" (Acts 9:15). Paul was made the Apostle to the Gentiles and given a gospel message specifically for them — the Gospel of Grace!

Paul now compares himself to the apostles in Jerusalem. His demeanor is straight to the point and sometimes appears brash, but he is defending his apostleship. His directness is sometimes offensive and not like the eloquence of these others who teach not the truth. Verses 5-6:

> 5 **For I suppose I was not a whit [speck] behind the very chiefest apostles.**

6 But though I be rude in speech, yet not in knowledge; but we have been throughly made manifest [open] among you in all things.

In what some may consider abrasiveness, Paul has always been open with the truth *in all things*; never hiding his purpose or his message.

Throughout his ministry, Paul worked as a tentmaker to supply his own needs. Other assemblies did send him support for his ministry. However, he did not want to be indebted to the Corinthians. He maintained his independence so that they could never say that the Gospel of Grace was not free. Verses 7-9:

7 Have I committed an offence in abasing myself that ye might be exalted, because I have preached to you the gospel of God freely?

8 I robbed other churches, taking wages of [from] them, to do you service.

9 And when I was present with you, and wanted [had needs], I was chargeable to no man: for that which was lacking to me the brethren which came from

Macedonia supplied: and in all things I have kept myself from being burdensome unto you, and so will I keep myself.

Other assemblies contributed to the meager care of their apostle. Macedonia made it possible to Paul to spend time teaching the believers at Corinth. Yet, from them, he asked for nothing.

There can be no question on their part concerning his love for them. Like a proud father boasts of his children, he does so throughout the regions of Achaia. Verses 10-11:

10 As the truth of Christ is in me, no man shall stop me of this boasting in the regions of Achaia. 11 Wherefore? [Why?] because I love you not? God knoweth [that I do].

The word *occasion* has an important meaning here. Its means *an event, happening, occurrence, or incident*. It is *something which is distinct from the ordinary course or orders of things*. These false teachers want the opportunity to take Paul's place and gain the same respect he garners. Verse 12:

12 But what I do, that I will do, that <u>I may</u>

cut off occasion from them which desire occasion; that wherein they glory [boast], [that] they may be found even as we [like us].

These others are prideful and boastful even to the point of believing themselves to be superior to Paul. They proclaim that he is inferior and not worthy of his apostolic office. As a result, Paul desires that they be cut off or prevented from any *occasion* or opportunity to teach error within the assembly.

These fake apostles are liars. They act on behalf of Satan to deceive those who are weak in the faith. For this reason, Paul sent Timothy and Titus to Corinth to strengthen their faith. Verses 13-15:

13 For such are **false apostles**, **deceitful workers**, transforming themselves into the apostles of Christ.

14 And no marvel [marvel not]; for Satan himself is transformed into an angel of light.

15 Therefore it is no great thing if his ministers also be transformed as the ministers of righteousness; **whose end shall be according to their works.**

Someday, those who deceive with false doctrines will receive an appropriate judgment from God.

Paul defends his apostleship. The cost of his apostleship was to suffer greatly throughout his ministry. Like a teacher, when Paul repeats something, we should pay attention. Verses 16-17:

> 16 **I say again, Let no man think me a fool; if otherwise, yet as a fool receive me, <u>that I may boast [about] myself a little.</u>**

> 17 **That which I speak, I speak it not after the Lord, but as it were foolishly, in this confidence of boasting.**

He considers it foolish for him to boast in the flesh, but wants them to know the cost of his apostleship. Below, Paul uses the word *suffer* to mean *allow or tolerate*. Verses 18-20:

> 18 **Seeing that many [others] glory after the flesh, I will glory also.**

> 19 **For ye suffer fools gladly, seeing ye yourselves are wise.**

> 20 **For ye suffer, if a man bring you into**

bondage, if a man devour you, if a man take of [from] you, if a man exalt himself, if a man smite you on the face.

The false teachers would chastise them, place them under the bondage of the Law, and take away their liberty. All the while, the Corinthians were *suffering* or *allowing* this to happen in their own assembly.

He speaks about *reproach* which means *the cause of shame or disgrace.* Whether it is the reproach non-believers are heaping upon the Corinthians or the debasement of his apostleship, they must not waiver. They must stand up for correct doctrine and not be weak or waffle. They must be bold. Correct doctrine must always be defended knowing it is the *Word of God.* The word *whereinsoever* means *in what ever matter, respect, or action.* Verse 21:

21 I speak as concerning reproach, as though we had been weak. Howbeit whereinsoever any is bold, (I speak foolishly,) I am bold also.

Be that as it may; in whatever situation we must be bold to defend the Word of God. In the following, Paul shares his own experiences with which few could compare. Verses 22-27:

22 Are they Hebrews? so am I. Are they Israelites? so am I. Are they the seed of Abraham? so am I.

23 Are they ministers of Christ? (I speak as a fool) I am more; in labours more abundant, in stripes above measure, in prisons more frequent, in deaths oft.

24 Of the Jews five times received I forty stripes save one. 25 Thrice was I beaten with rods, once was I stoned, thrice I suffered shipwreck, a night and a day I have been in the deep; 26 In journeyings often, in perils of waters, in perils of robbers, in perils by mine own country-men, in perils by the heathen, in perils in the city, in perils in the wilderness, in perils in the sea, in perils among false brethren;

27 In weariness and painfulness, in watchings often, in hunger and thirst, in fastings often, in cold and naked-ness.

To all this, he must add the weight of care and concern for the believers. Verses 28-29:

28 Beside those things that are without [outside], that which cometh upon me daily, [there is also] the care of all the churches.

29 Who is weak, and I am not weak? who is offended, and I burn not?

As a man, Paul acknowledges his weakness. However, in his weakness, he has learned to rely on God Who watches over him. God gives him his strength. It is God Who provides for Paul far beyond his own frail abilities. He depends upon God. Therefore, if he must glory, he will glory in God. Verses 30-31:

30 If I must needs glory, I will glory of the things which concern mine infirmities.

31 The God and Father of our Lord Jesus Christ, which is blessed for evermore, knoweth that I lie not.

Here is another example of how God saved Paul's life. Luke records the story of this treachery against him in Acts 9:23-25:

23 And after that many days were fulfilled, the Jews took counsel to kill him:

24 But their laying await was known of Saul. And they watched the gates day and night to kill him. **25** Then the disciples took him by night, and let him down by the wall in a basket.

Speaking of Paul, God told Ananias, "For I will shew him how great things he must suffer for my name's sake" (Acts 9:16). Paul closes this chapter by making reference to the above event. 2 Corinthians 11:32-33:

32 In Damascus the governor under Aretas the king kept the city of the Damascenes with a garrison, desirous to apprehend me:

33 And through a window in a basket was I let down by the wall, and escaped his hands.

We know that Paul's life was filled with adversities. Yet, God continually showed His providential care to the Apostle of Grace.

13

2 Corinthians 12

Here are a couple words we must consider. The first word is *expedient* which means *the urging or pushing forward, promoting or advancing something.* The second word is *doubtless* which means *unquestionable or without any doubt.* Paul says that, without question, it is neither useful nor beneficial for believers to glory in their own experiences. He cites himself as an example. In spite of his role as an apostle, he does not boast. He continues by sharing certain visions and revelations he received from the Lord. 2 Corinthians 12:1-4:

> 1 **It is not expedient for me doubtless to glory. <u>I will come to visions and revelations of the Lord</u>.**

> 2 I knew a man in Christ above fourteen years ago, (whether in the body, I cannot tell; or whether out of the body, I cannot tell: God knoweth;) such an one caught up to the third heaven.

> 3 And I knew such a man, (whether in the body, or out of the body, I cannot tell: God knoweth;)

> 4 How that he was caught up into paradise, and heard unspeakable words, which it is not lawful for a man to utter.

It is my belief that this man of whom he speaks was indeed himself. In order to not glorify himself, he speaks in the third person. He cannot confirm whether this happened in the body or in the spirit. He leaves the reader to consider something that he says only the Lord knows.

Having this experience, Paul glories in his own *infirmities* – his weaknesses and frailties. Verses 5-6:

> 5 Of such an one will I glory: yet of myself I will not glory, but in mine infirmities.

> 6 For though I would desire to glory, I

**shall not be a fool; for I will say the
truth: but now I forbear, lest any man
should think of me above that which he
seeth me to be, or that he heareth of me.**

He constrains himself as he recounts this event, so
that no one would think more highly of him. To prevent Paul from being overwhelmed with this glorious revelation, the Lord allowed something to happen to him. God's purposed to keep Paul earthly
grounded. He explains this in verse 7:

> **7 And lest [So that] I should be exalted
> above measure through the abundance
> of the revelations, there was given to me
> a thorn in the flesh, the messenger of
> Satan to buffet me, lest I should be exalted above measure.**

This would be one of the infirmities in which Paul
gloried. Some believe that this *thorn in the flesh* was a
health issue affecting his eyesight. This left him unable to write his own letters. He used a scribe.

Paul prayed three times to the Lord requesting
healing. He did receive an answer. Verses 8-9:

> **8 For [Concerning] this thing I besought
> the Lord thrice [three times], that it [this**

infirmity] might depart from me.

9 And he said unto me, <u>My grace is sufficient for thee: for my strength is made perfect in weakness.</u> Most gladly therefore will I rather glory in my infirmities, that the power of Christ may rest upon me.

The answer he received was "no." We can ask God anything. He is all-knowing and has the right to decide the response according to His will. Paul shares his own lessons with other grace believers. Verse 10:

10 Therefore I take pleasure in infirmities, in reproaches, in necessities, in persecutions, in distresses for Christ's sake: for when I am weak, then [in Christ] am I strong.

It is the current state of the Corinthian assembly that compels him to address their situation. 2 Corinthians 12:11-12:

11 I am become a fool in glorying; ye have compelled me: for I ought to have been commended of you: <u>for in nothing am I behind the very chiefest apostles,</u> though I be nothing.

12 Truly the signs [evidence] of an apostle were wrought among you in all patience, in signs, and wonders, and mighty deeds.

He continues to defend his apostleship by comparing it to the chief apostle of the Twelve. Yet, in humility, he considers himself nothing. He recalls the beginning of his ministry during which time his apostleship was confirmed by *signs, and wonders, and mighty deeds.* These were necessary for the Jews who require miracles, signs, and wonders for authentication. Later in his ministry, he told the Corinthians that ". . . we walk by faith, not by sight" (2 Cor. 5:7).

Paul asks the Corinthians what makes them different from the other assemblies? Here, he was not a financial burden to them. He supported himself by working and the gifts he received from the other assemblies. Verse 13:

13 For what is it wherein ye were inferior to other churches, except it be that I myself was not burdensome to you? forgive me this wrong.

Paul is making plans to come to Corinth again and, even in that visit, he plans not to burden them with the costs. Verses 14-15:

14 Behold, the third time I am ready to come to you; and I will not be burdensome to you: for I seek not [what is] yours, but you: for the children ought not to lay up for the parents, but the parents for the children.

15 And I will very gladly spend and be spent for you; though the more abundantly I love you, the less I be loved.

He will gladly pour himself out for them if it will bear fruit. However, it appears that the more he loves them, the less he is loved by them.

Paul tests them and finds in them *guile*. The word *guile* means *crafty, cunning, artifice, or deceit.* He is accusing them of duplicity or double-dealing. They act one way with Paul and another way in his absence. Verses 16-18:

16 But be it so, I did not burden you: nevertheless, being crafty, I caught you with guile. 17 Did I make a gain of you by any of them whom I sent unto you?

18 I desired Titus, and with him I sent a brother. Did Titus make a gain of you? walked we not in the same spirit? walk-

ed we not in the same steps?

Neither Paul nor the two teachers he sent after him made any gain or improvement in them. All of them had the same spirit of giving in love to *edify* them. Here the word *edify* means *to instruct or teach them in faith and holiness.*

As the Apostle to the Gentiles, Paul was given the responsibility of overseeing the proclamation of the *Gospel of Grace*. His desire is to edify believers by teaching them in faith and holiness. In all that he does, it is done *before God Who* is a witness of his work in this ministry. Verse 19:

> 19 **Again, think ye that we excuse our-selves unto you? we speak before God in Christ: but we do all things, dearly beloved, for your edifying.**

He hopes to find that they have turned from their sins. He is afraid he will find that is not the case when he comes to them. If so, it will require that he deal with the matter in person. His letter was written in love as if from the father of their faith. How they respond to this letter will determine how he will be with them on his next visit. Verses 20-21:

20 For I fear, lest, when I come, I shall

not find you such as I would [hope], and that I shall be found unto you such as ye would not: lest there be debates, envyings, wraths, strifes, backbitings, whisperings, swellings, tumults:

21 And lest, when I come again, my God will humble me among you, and that I shall bewail many which have sinned already, and have not repented of [turned from] the uncleanness and fornication and lasciviousness which they have committed.

14

2 Corinthians 13

Paul plans on making his third visit to Corinth to meet with the believers there. When he gets there he will use the testimony of two or three to establish the state of the assembly. 2 Corinthians 13:1:

> 1 **This is the third time I am coming to you. In the mouth of two or three witnesses shall every word be established.**

In the letter, he writes to both those who are in sin and those who are not. If he comes to them, then he will not hesitate to rebuke them. This should be proof that it is not him speaking, but Christ Who speaking through him. Verses 2-3:

> 2 **I told you before, and foretell you, as if I were present, the second time; and**

being absent now I write to them which heretofore have sinned, and to all other, that, if I come again, I will not spare:

3 Since ye seek a proof of Christ speaking in me, which to you-ward is not weak, but is mighty in you.

He teaches about the weakness in individuals and the strength of God. He uses Christ as an example. While on earth, Christ was a man with all the frailty and weakness inherent in all men. Verse 4:

4 For though he was crucified through weakness, yet he liveth by the power of God. For we also are weak in him, but we shall live with him by the power of God toward you.

This weakness is our fallen state on earth. Our flesh is weak. Therefore, it is not by our strength, but by the power of God revealed in us.

Paul calls upon the Corinthians to examine themselves as no one else would be better. Their beliefs and actions must reflect Christ in them. Some abandoned Paul's teaching. Those chose to believe error taught by others. They are *reprobates* and are not saved. Verses 5-6:

5 **Examine yourselves, whether ye be in the faith; prove your own selves. Know ye not your own selves, how that Jesus Christ is in you, except ye be reprobates?**

6 **But I trust that ye shall know that we are not reprobates.**

He reminds those who are saved by grace have Christ in them. He is confident they know that he and his fellow workers are not reprobates.

He continues this thought. He asks God that the Corinthians do no evil. All believers should do nothing contrary to the truth of God, but in all things support it. Verses 7-8:

7 **Now I pray to God that ye do no evil; not that we should appear approved, but that ye should do that which is honest, though we be as reprobates.**

8 **For we can do nothing against the truth, but for the truth.**

He encourages believers to be honest with themselves. Paul and his fellow workers can do nothing against the truth; only for the truth.

Paul compares weakness and strength saying that weakness is human while strength is God. His desire is that they work towards being like Christ. Believers cannot be perfect in their weakness. Otherwise, there would have been no need for the Cross. Still, Paul expects all believers to strive to be more like Christ. Verses 9-10:

> 9 **For we are glad, when we are weak, and ye are strong: and this also we wish, even [that is to say for] your perfection.**

> 10 **Therefore I write these things being absent, lest being present I should use sharpness, according to the power which the Lord hath given me to edification, and not to destruction.**

As their apostle, he wants to encourage them by edifying their faith and not destroying it. When he comes to them, he desires that all of them will be accepted in the Lord. He gives them a charge or challenge. He wants them to prosper in their faith. Verse 11:

> 11 **Finally, brethren, farewell. Be perfect, be of good comfort, be of one mind, live in peace; and the God of love and peace shall be with you.**

It is an Eastern tradition to press the opposite side of each cheek together as a kiss. This was a customary greeting within the fellowship of believers. Verses 12-13:

> 12 **Greet one another with an holy kiss.**
> 13 **All the saints salute you.**

He closes with this blessing. Verses 14:

> 14 **The grace of the Lord Jesus Christ, and the love of God, and the communion of the Holy Ghost, be with you all. Amen.**

Epilogue

Let us imagine, for a moment, all assemblies must have a semiannual audit done by God. Paul will be sent to each assembly for two weeks. While he is there, he will talk to every believer, attend the services and join the activities. Once his assessment is complete, the assembly will receive a report card like those given to students. Paul does not write a letter of condemnation to the Corinthians. He writes one that edifies the believers. In his closing, believers are encouraged to rejoice in the grace of the Lord Jesus Christ and the love of God. They are to fellowship together in the blessings of the Holy Spirit.

Paul desires that all believers complete a self-assessment. No one knows us better than we do ourselves. You might ask, "What would be the standard by which we all should make this assessment?" Today, we have the completed Scripture. This is the measure by which we should compare ourselves; not one to another. There are standards by which God expects us to live. Paul outlined these in his letter. The assembly of believers are representatives of Christ. Therefore, its reputation in the community is important. Anything that tarnishes the image of Christ, most notably fornication, should not be tolerated. For the Corinthians, it was their lack of the response that was a greater problem. All believers with blatant open sin within the assembly must not be tolerated. It is bad for the believers, but far worse as a testimony to non-believers.

Paul addressed this issue in his first letter. He tells them that he has withheld strong words in his writing. He desires for them to correct the situation themselves before he comes to them in person. He wrote, "Therefore I write these things being absent, lest being present I should use sharpness, according to the power which the Lord hath given me to edification, and not to destruction" (2 Cor 13: 10).

There were those within the assembly who teach false doctrine. They deny Paul's apostolic office and teach the necessity of adding works to the *Gospel of Grace*. This was a common problem then as much as it is in today's churches. The assembly at Corinth was the largest of all the assemblies. Their financial means far exceeded the others. In his letters to them, Paul does not use condemnation. He encourages towards his desire that they become an exemplary assembly. They are more than capable as they are already *in Christ*. He never asked for support while he lived among them. In this way, they could never say that the *Gospel of Grace* came to them at a cost. In the future, Paul hopes they will want to participate in the *ministry of reconciliation* with a spirit of generosity.

In his second letter, Paul displays his great love and care for the believers. He gave to the Corinthians and, for that matter, all grace believers his instruction for living. Christ has done everything we need for the final redemption of our bodies, the Rapture. Then, we will be complete *in Christ*. We have the holy Spirit of Promise as our guaranty. (*cf.* Eph. 1:13-14.) While we remain on earth waiting for this event, we are being sanctified. The work of separating believers from the world is called our *sanctification*. It is the process by which Christ separates us from the world.

Sanctification feels like a long and arduous process. However, there is good news. It is a process which is undertaken by God within every grace believer. The Holy Spirit resides in each of us. God Himself will complete the task. When Paul writes to the assembly in Philippi, he explains that our sanctification will be completed by God before *His Calling* or the Rapture. Philippians 1:3-6:

> 3 **I thank my God upon every remem-brance of you,** 4 **Always in every prayer of mine for you all making request with joy,**

> 5 **For your fellowship in the gospel from the first day until now;**

> 6 <u>**Being confident of this very thing, that he [God] which hath begun a good work in you will perform it until the day of Jesus Christ.**</u>

This *Day of Jesus Christ* is the day when He appears in the clouds to call the Body of Christ unto Himself. Our sanctification will be complete before we are raptured. We know this from Ephesians 5:27:

> 27 **That he might present it to himself a glorious church, not having spot, or wrinkle, or any such thing; but that it should be holy and without blemish.**

We can be confident in this. God, through His Son, completed the work necessary to secure our *justification*. We have the righteousness of Christ impressed upon us as believers saved by His grace alone. As we sojourn on earth, we wait for His Calling. Before that happens, God will complete our *sanctification.* That will separate us from the world and only unto Him. Then, on the *Day of Jesus Christ,* it is Christ, Christ will call us to Himself. It is He Who will complete our redemption. We will receive bodies like His. That will be our *glorification.* We will be with Him forever in glory.

At present, we are undergoing our sanctification. Paul explains the process which God is undertaking within us now. Romans 8:16-17:

> 16 **The Spirit itself beareth witness with our spirit, that <u>we are the children of God</u>:**
>
> 17 **And if children, then heirs; heirs of God, and joint-heirs with Christ; <u>if so be that we suffer with him, that we may be also glorified together.</u>**

Did you notice the words *if so be that we suffer with him?* These struggles, trials, and tribulations we are experiencing here on earth are all part of separating us from the world. We are to suffer like He did while on earth to be glorified with Him. Therefore, what we are experiencing here on earth is actually God separating us unto Himself for eternity!

It is my hope that you enjoyed reading this book and have a better understanding of the Apostle Paul and his Gospel of Grace for this present age.

Sinner saved by grace,
Dr. David Alan Greene

Other GraceWord Publications

Cartas A Teofilo
Efesios: Dispensacionalmente considerado
El evangelio Oculto: Una vez fue un misterio . . .

About The Author

Dr. David Alan Greene has over thirty-five years of experience as an insurance agent selling both property and casualty as well as life insurance. During his career, he taught and explained the content and meaning of policies to his clients. Now retired, he devotes much of his time to teaching the Bible.

He obtained his Bachelor of Theology, Master of Biblical Studies, and Ph.D. in Biblical Studies from Evangelical Theological Seminary where he holds the position of Dean of Graduate Studies. He also holds a Ph.D. in Christian Counseling. He has written numerous biblical commentaries and books on rightly dividing the Word of Truth.